D1707215

FORETOLD

THE COVID-19 EFFECT

THE CALM BEFORE THE STORM
OF BIBLICAL PROPHETIC EVENTS

TONY BOSSERMAN

Concord Press
Loomis, CA

Concord Press/Foretold
Cover Design: Joel Bosserman
Printer: R. R. Donnelley

Foretold/ Anthony Bosserman -- 1st ed.

ISBN 978-0-578-76421-4 Print Edition

CONTENTS

To YAH, the ONLY TRUE GOD, whose word lies within these pages, inspired by HIS HOLY SPIRIT.

FOREWORD

Imagine you were hiking in the Himalayan Mountains, and no-ticed a shiny object on the ground, and after a little excavation, you unearthed a lockbox containing an ancient book. As you opened the book and began perusing its pages, you were intrigued by a particular text about some ethereal beings descending out of the sky on horseback in some kind of reconnaissance mission to find out why the Earth's Nations had suddenly become quiet and at rest. Well, you'd probably be amused, but mostly you'd be wondering if the book had any market value as a relic.

But when you descended the mountains with this precious ar-chaeological find, and turned on the television, you were stunned to learn that a pestilence called COVID 19 had become pandemic. The world's commerce and social interaction had all but stopped, and there was an eerie silence enveloping the entire earth. So you re-opened this lock-box book with august, read that text again, confirmed what you remembered, and looked to see if there were any details you missed. Only to find in your 2nd reading of the text, that the foretelling of this event was given in the very season of the year that this 'cloak of silence' had descended upon Human Civilization!

How would you feel? Well probably astounded! And you would immediately want to show the book to members of the Media, World Leaders, and Religious gurus, to spread the word and tell all Humanity that **an ancient book FORETOLD the COVID-19 EFFECT of silencing and bringing to rest the entire world!**

That ancient book is your Bible – and it contains hundreds of adumbrations that have come to pass just as they were **FORETOLD**!

The re-planting of Israel as a nation is something that was **FORETOLD** in over a dozen prophecies of the Old Testament! Israel's acquisition of the West Bank and the Sinai Peninsula during the Yom-Kippur 1967 war - was also **FORETOLD**!

A war in Syria is leading to the demise of Damascus as a city and the exile of over a million Syrians into modern-day Jordan – this too was **FORETOLD** - history written in advance!

The rise and fall of ISIS dumfounded the world, but your Bible **FORETOLD** of this coming calamitous war machine centuries ago!

And yes this ancient book of the Hebrews also **FORETOLD**, 2500 years in advance, that one day **all the earth would be resting quietly** - and that Angelic beings would come down on horseback and record the event firsthand!

This is the 1st of 8 visions given to the prophet Zechariah, and it's the calm before the storm of Biblical prophetic events to come! What's coming next? Read on – and you'll get a glimpse into the prophetic portrait outlined in the pages of your Bible by the greatest Political Forecaster ever – ALMIGHTY GOD!

And fulfilling many prophecies from the Biblical page, GOD replanted Israel on the world stage, in 1948. (JER.30:3)

If the Cosmos was chaos without any order, if there were no cycles nor systems nor borders, one might believe things could happen by chance, but not the design we see in the expanse (JOB 37:14). Cycles of flowers (Song of Solomon 2:12-13), and birds (JEREMIAH 8:7) and seasons (GENESIS 1:14), systems in our bodies (PSALM 139:14), and mind and reason (JOB 38:36) – must come from ONE who always has been, who has the power to also transcend (PHILIPPIANS 4:7).

It has not been shown how LAW can evolve, yet Science admits that everything revolves, whether astral bodies, or living cells, by invisible RULES with unbending resolve. There is ONE LAW-GIVER (JA.4:12) who keeps everything in motion, the sun, moon, and stars declare their devotion (PS.148:3)

There are secret things which GOD revealed (DT.29:29), not verified till the 'modern age,' like why living things produce only their kind (GENESIS 1:11,12,20) – it's written in their DNA.

Thousands of years before Modern Medicine knew, Biblical writers revealed unknown truths: like the fact that ribs can regenerate anew (GEN.2:21); Quarantine of disease keeps it to the few (LEV.13:46) and that animal saliva is harmful goo (EXODUS 22:31). Your Bible reveals that sanitation is wise (DEUT.23:12,13) (LEV.15:13); that blood clotting peaks on the 8th day of life (LEVITICUS 12:3); and that life is in the blood, to manys' surprise (LEVITICUS 17:11). Did you know that Scripture reveals 'air' has weight (JOB 28:25)? that the Oceans have currents (PS.8:8) and subterranean lakes (JOB 38:16)? Make no mistake, these things were revealed through THE DIVINE SAGE, millennia before 'the Modern Age.'

Only 'the fool' says in his heart, 'There is no GOD,' (PSALM 14:1) when there's proof a' la Carte. The menu includes all of these items: Design, Law, and Order – any many besides them. No other book reveals such truths, of past, present, future with accurate   views. You've seen the evidence – now you must choose: ETERNAL LIFE or eternal lose... (DEUTERONOMY 30:19).

CHAPTER 1
THE REPLANTING OF ISRAEL

Jesus' disciples once asked Him, "**What will be the sign of your coming, and of the end of the Age?**" Jesus answered with a lengthy dissertation that has come to be called 'The Olivet Prophecy:'

> "Take heed that no one deceives you. For many will come in My name, saying, 'I am the Christ,' and will deceive many. And you will hear of wars and rumors of wars. See that you are not troubled; for all these things must come to pass, but the end is not yet. For **nation** (GK. 'Ethnos' = Race, Tribe, **Ethnic group**) **shall rise up against nation** (**Ethnic Group**), and kingdom against kingdom. And there will be famines, **pestilences**, and earthquakes in various places. **All these are the beginning of sorrows**." (MATTHEW 24:4-8 NKJV)

What do we see happening all over the world today? Ethnic group is rising up against Ethnic group – not just in the United States, with 'Black Lives Matter' riots across the Country – but on every continent: The Chinese have incarcerated up to a million Uyghurs in camps that sound disturbingly like the 'Concentration

Camps' of Nazi Germany; Turks and Kurds are at war with one another; Iraqi's would like to see the Yazidis removed from their soil; Pakistani's and Indians are at constant odds with one another; Strife is building between Ethiopia's Oromos, Somalis, and Gedeos; There's an on-going conflict between the Aboriginals and white population of Australia; There's continued tension between Croats and Serbs in Europe, and Indigenous peoples of Central and South America remain in conflict with their countrymen of European descent.

That's just the tip of the iceberg – there are hundreds of 'Ethnic Conflicts' raging all over the world today!

As we watch world news, we also see famines, pestilences, and earthquakes accompanying these Ethnic and Kingdom Conflicts. But as Jesus says, these are only '**the beginning of sorrows**.'

Continuing in the 'Olivet Prophecy,' we read:

"Therefore when you see the '**abomination of desolation**' spoken of by Daniel the Prophet, **standing in the Holy Place** (whoever reads let him understand), then let those who are in Judea flee to the mountains. Let him who is on the housetop not go down to take anything out of his house. And let him who is in the field not go back to get his clothes. But woe to those who are pregnant and to those who are nursing babies in those days! And pray that your flight may not be in winter or on the Sabbath. **For then there will be GREAT TRIBULATION**, such as has not been since the beginning of the world until this time, no, nor ever shall be. **And unless those days were shortened, no flesh would be saved**; but for the Elect's sake those days will be shortened." (MATTHEW 24:15-22 NKJV)

This 'abomination of desolation', according to Daniel the Prophet, is set up (HEB. 'Nathan' fasten, lift up) when the 'daily sacrifice' in Israel is taken away (DANIEL 12:11).

To understand why this event launches the whole world into the most significant time of trouble in Human History, we have to go back to the beginning and find out why **Israel becomes the epicenter of 'End Time Events.'**

CONCEPTION of a NATION

In a world re-arranged by a worldwide flood, and the dispersal of the survivors to the far flung areas of the earth at Babel (GENESIS 11) - GOD chose to isolate a man and his household from his kin and make him a nomad in other nation's lands. His name was Abram, and because he was willing to obey GOD'S voice, keep HIS charge, HIS commandments, HIS statutes, and HIS laws (GENESIS 26:5), GOD made a promise to him that HE made with no other Human Being before or since:

> "Get out of your Country, from your family and from your father's house, to a Land that I will show you. **I will make you a great nation**; I will bless you and make your name great; And you shall be a blessing. **I will bless those who bless you**, **and I will curse him who curses you**; And **in you all the families of the earth shall be blessed**." (GENESIS 12:1-3 NKJV)

One of the logical questions that comes out of the reading of this text, is how exactly has this man's descendants blessed all the families of the earth? The spiritual answer to that question is: the pardon of all men's sins through the death of one of Abram's descendants, Jesus 'the Christ' of Nazareth (EPHESIANS 1:7).

The physical answers to that question are multitudinous: A system of Law and Ethics that the Christian nations of Western Civilization have very much incorporated in their executive, legislative and judicial branches of government; a book called the Bible that adds to the Historical insight of many peoples throughout the Middle East; Some of the most extraordinary scientific and literary contributions to Humanity have come from Jewish winners of Nobel prizes, who represent only 0.2% of the world's population, yet have won 20% of the prizes given!

Through this man's seed came not only the future nation of Israel but the Arab peoples of the Middle East as well. Many people are familiar with the 12 Tribes of Israel – but are not aware of the 12 Tribes of Ishmael:

> "And as for **Ishmael** (Abraham's son through a 2nd wife), I (The Lord) have heard you. Behold, I have blessed him and will make him fruitful, and will multiply him exceedingly. **He shall beget 12 Princes, and I will make of him a great nation**. But MY covenant I will establish with Isaac, whom Sarah (Abram's wife) shall bear to you at this set time next year." (GENESIS 17:20,21 NKJV)

The world has also been incredibly blessed through these Arab descendants of Abram as well: Arab nations hold 43% of the world's oil reserves and produce nearly 1/3 of the world's oil supply; The 10th Century Arab Muslim, Qasim Al Zahrawi, is called the 'Father of Surgery,' having invented the Scalpel, surgical scissors, and the surgical needle; Arab Physicist Hasan Ibn Al-Haythem (965-1045 A.D.) is referred to by many as the 'Father of Optics.'

Volumes could be filled by the contributions made by the Israeli and Arab peoples that have 'blessed' the world – just as GOD promised their shared father, Abram!

Isaac was a child of promise from GOD through a barren wife who was 90 years old! Abraham and Sarah had to wait 25 years for a son from the fruit of their union, knowing they would never see the formation of the nation of Israel he would become.

Besides having to leave his homeland, become a nomad for the rest of his life, and wait 25 years for an heir through whom the promise of nationhood would come – Abraham was told that his descendants, through Isaac, would first have to endure centuries of slavery:

"Then HE said to Abram: 'Know certainly that your descendants will be strangers in a land that is not theirs, and will serve them, and they will afflict them 400 years. And also the nation whom they serve (**Egypt**), I will judge; afterward they shall come out with great possessions." (GENESIS 15:13,14 NKJV)

The descendants of this great spiritual giant gestated 400 years in the womb of Egypt, growing into a nation of 600,000 men (EXODUS 12:37 NKJV) besides women and children (making a population of 2-3 million total).

But there came a day for this nation to depart from its mother and be born into this world as an independent Nation:

"Now the sojourn of the children of Israel who lived in Egypt was 430 years (**30 years in freedom under their brother Joseph and 400 years under Pharaohs who enslaved them**). And it came to pass at the end of the 430 years – on that very same day – it came to pass that all the armies of the Lord went out from the Land of Egypt." (EX.12:40,41)

So a Country can be born in a day, a Nation brought forth in a moment! (ISAIAH 66:8) Israel began as a nomadic Nation, but eventually dispossessed the peoples of the Land of Canaan.

PLUCKING and PLANTING

Critics of the GOD of the Bible ask why HE would allow, encourage, and facilitate one nation to take another nation's land. Our CREATOR gives the answer through these two texts of the Bible:

"The instant I speak concerning **a nation** and concerning a kingdom, **to pluck up**, **to pull down**, **and to destroy it**, if that nation against whom I have spoken turns from its evil, I will relent of the disaster that I thought to bring upon it. And the instant I speak concerning **a nation** and concerning a kingdom, **to build and to plant it**, if it does evil in MY SIGHT so that it does not obey MY VOICE, then I will relent concerning the good with which I said I would benefit it." (JEREMIAH 18:7-10 NKJV)

"When you (Israelites) come into the Land which THE LORD your GOD is giving you, you shall not learn to follow the abominations of those nations. There shall not be found among you **anyone who makes his son or his daughter pass through the fire**, **or one who practices witchcraft**, or **a soothsayer**, or **one who interprets omens**, **or a sorcerer** or **one who conjures spells**, or **a medium**, or **a spiritist**, **or one who calls up the dead**. For all who do these things are an abomination to THE LORD, and **because of these abominations** THE LORD your GOD **drives them** (the Canaanites) **out from before you**." (DEUTERONOMY 18:9-12)

ALMIGHTY GOD gave the Canaanites 400 years to repent, while Israel was forming in the womb of Egypt." (GENESIS 15:16) But they did not repent. Instead, they became more corrupt. So GOD supplanted them with the descendants of Abraham as their punishment.

And being THE EQUITABLE GOD HE IS – THE MOST HIGH supplanted Israel with peoples hand chosen by their conqueror (II KINGS 17:26,27), when they wouldn't turn from their evil, after being supernaturally planted in the Land of Canaan.

The nation of Jordan is one of many countries in the Middle East that condemns Israel for what they feel is the supplanting of earlier people's lands. Yet the Bible is clear that the nation of Jordan (descendants of Ammon, Moab, and Esau) supplanted the indigenous peoples of their land:

"Then THE LORD said to me (Moses), 'Do not harass Moab (Central Jordan today), nor contend with them in battle, for I will not give you any of their land as a possession, because I have given Ar to the descendants of Lot (Abram's nephew) as a possession.' (**The E'mim had dwelt there in times past**)… **The Horites formerly dwelt in Seir** (Southern Jordan today), **but the descendants of Esau dispossessed them**… And when you come near the people of Ammon (Northern Jordan today), do not harass them or meddle with them, for I will not give you any of the land of the people of Ammon as a possession, because I have given it to the descendants of Lot as a possession. (That was also regarded as a land of giants; giants formerly dwelt there. But the Ammonites call them '**Zam-zum'mim**,' a people as great and numerous and tall as the An'a-kim. But THE LORD destroyed them before them, and **they** (the Ammonites) **dispossessed them and dwelt in their place**." (DEUTERONOMY 2:9-12; 19-21 NKJV)

This double standard is never cited by the Western Press when referring to Israel's 'stolen lands.'

The uprooting of Israel as a nation and supplanting of its lands by foreigners had to be temporary however because THE CREATOR GOD had made a promise to Abraham:

"THE LORD said to Abram, after Lot had separated from him: 'Lift your eyes now and look from the place where you are – northward, southward, eastward and westward; for **all the land which you see I give to you and your descendants forever**. (GEN.13:14,15)

"Are you not our GOD, who drove out the inhabitants of this land before YOUR people Israel and **gave it to the descendants of Abraham YOUR friend forever**?" (II CHRONICLES 20:7)

Several empires have occupied the Land of Israel over the centuries – but it has never become another Nation-State. National disobedience led to Israel's temporary supplanting, but GOD ALMIGHTY always brings HIS people back to their Land:

"Therefore thus says THE LORD of HOSTS: 'Because you (Israel) have not heard MY words, behold, I will send and take all the families of the North,' says THE LORD, 'and Nebuchadnezzar the King of Babylon, MY servant and will bring them against this Land… And this whole land shall be a desolation and an astonishment, and these nations shall **serve the King of Babylon 70 years**. Then it will come to pass, when

70 years are completed, that I will punish the King of Babylon and that nation, the land of the Chaldeans, for their iniquity..." (JEREMIAH 25:8,9,11,12 NKJV)

Israel's captivity was to be 70 years long, and then their Captor (The Babylonians) would also be punished for their sins. But GOD also said that Israel would return to their lands and their temple would be rebuilt – and HE even named the King who would decree it – a century in advance:

"...Who says of **Cyrus** (the great), 'He is MY shepherd, and he shall perform all MY pleasure, saying to Jerusalem, '**You shall be built**,' and to the temple, '**Your foundation shall be laid**.'" (ISAIAH 44:28 NKJV)

Now in the first year of Cyrus King of Persia, that the word of THE LORD by the mouth of Jeremiah might be fulfilled, **THE LORD stirred up the spirit of Cyrus King of Persia**, so that he made a proclamation throughout all his kingdom, and also put it in writing, saying, 'Thus says Cyrus king of Persia: All the kingdoms of the earth THE LORD GOD of HEAVEN has given me. And **HE has commanded me to build HIM a house at Jerusalem which is in Judah**. Who is among you of all HIS people? May his GOD be with him, and let him go up to Jerusalem which is in Judah, and build the house of THE LORD GOD of Israel (HE is GOD), which is in Jerusalem. And whoever is left in any place where he dwells, let the men of his place help him with silver and gold, with goods and livestock, besides the freewill offerings for the house of GOD which is in Jerusalem." (EZRA 1:1-4 NKJV)

Isaiah, the prophet, lived and wrote a century in advance of Cyrus' birth – yet THE GOD of HEAVEN inspired him to name the man who would REPLANT Israel as a Nation back in their Land. Then HE commanded this secular leader of a different religion to write a decree to make it happen - a series of unprecedented events in Human History! Two whole books in your Bible relate the history of how this was carried out: the books of Ezra and Nehemiah – give them a read!

Centuries later, Israel's sins once again led to the destruction of the temple, and their disbursement from the land promised to them through Abraham. This was prophesied in what is famously called THE 70 WEEKS PROPHECY, in a vision given to Daniel the prophet:

"Seventy weeks are determined for your people and for your holy city, to finish the transgression, to make an end of sins, to make reconciliation for iniquity, to bring in everlasting righteousness, to seal up vision and prophecy, and to anoint the Most Holy. Know therefore and understand, that from the going forth of the command to restore and build **Jerusalem** (**Artaxerxes – EZRA 7:21-26**), until Messiah the Prince (Jesus), there shall be 7 weeks and 62 weeks; the street shall be built again, and the wall, even in troublesome times (described in the books of Ezra and Nehemiah). And after the 62 weeks Messiah shall be cut off, but not for Himself (but Humanity – II CORINTHIANS 5:15); And the people of a prince who is to come (Roman General Titus 70 A.D.) **shall destroy the city** (Jerusalem) **and the sanctuary** (the Temple). The end of it shall be with a flood (Armies: ISAIAH 28:20), and till the end of the war desolations are determined." (DANIEL 9:24-26 NKJV)

69 weeks times 7 days in a week equals 483 days. Obviously there were more than 483 days between Artaxerxes decree to let Israel rebuild Jerusalem and the death of the Messiah, so the 'day for a year' formula (EZEKIEL 4:5,6) must be intended here, meaning **a time period of 483 years**.

As anyone who studies history knows, the records of kings and their successors is not always complete or extant. That being said, Historians put the date of Artaxerxes decree at 457 B.C. So subtracting 483 years from 457 B.C. brings us to 26 A.D. and the Ministry of Christ. Remember that the '70 weeks prophecy' tells us that Messiah is cut off after the 62 weeks, which follows the 7 weeks or 483 years. It doesn't say precisely when His death would take place – but 'after' the 483 years – which occurred somewhere between 30-33 A.D.

The point in quoting the '70 weeks prophecy' is to show that once again, Israel was to be punished by GOD for their sins: Jerusalem and its temple were to be destroyed by a secular nation (History tells us it was Titus of Rome), and the Jews were once again **PLUCKED UP** from their land. While some Jews remained in the land, their sovereignty over it had long before disappeared, and now the center of their religious worship and rituals of sacrifice made to cease.

In a final revolt against the Roman Empire, the Jews rallied under the leadership of Simon Bar Kokhba in 135/6 A.D. but were soundly defeated. Emperor Hadrian expelled most of the Jews from Judaea, renamed the area 'Syria Palaestina,' and forbade Jews from entering Jerusalem.

But remember that the land of Israel still belonged to the descendants of Abraham's son Isaac, and there has always been a remnant of Jews living in that land down through the centuries. And the GOD of Israel made several promises to **REPLANT ISRAEL** in the future:

> "It shall come to pass, that **as I have watched over them** (Israel) **to pluck up**, to break down, to throw down, to destroy, and to afflict, so **I will watch over them to build and to plant**, says THE LORD." (JEREMIAH 31:28 NKJV)

> "Therefore behold, the days are coming, says THE LORD, that it shall no more be said, 'THE LORD LIVES who brought up the children of Israel from the land of Egypt,' but, 'THE LORD LIVES who brought up the children of Israel from the land of the North and from all the lands where HE had driven them.' **For I will bring them back into their land which I gave to their fathers**." (JEREMIAH 16:14,15 NKJV)

In 1922, the predecessor of the United Nations called the 'League of Nations,' gave Great Britain the mandate of control over the lands of Ancient Israel. On May 14th 1948, Great Britain withdrew her mandate, and Israel was declared a Sovereign State. The State of Israel was literally born once again in 'a day' as the Bible declared in a rhetorical question (ISAIAH 66:8).

The GREAT CREATOR GOD kept HIS promises and gathered Israelites from all over the world, replanting HIS people as a Sovereign Nation, after 2000 years of exile. This monumental event should have established in the minds of all that the GOD of the Bible is GOD and HIS word is truth!

But instead of returning to their GOD with all their hearts, minds, and souls, the modern 'State of Israel' has followed in the sins of all the nations of the earth over the last 70 years. Therefore She will once more be punished and lose her sovereignty:

"For behold, the days are coming, says THE LORD, that I will bring back from captivity MY people Israel and Judah,' says THE LORD. And I will cause them to return to the land that I gave to their fathers, and they shall possess it.' Now these are the words that THE LORD spoke concerning Israel and Judah. For thus says THE LORD: 'We have heard a voice of trembling, of fear, and not of peace. Ask now, and see, whether a man is ever in labor with child? So why do I see every man with his hands on his loins like a woman in labor, and all faces turned pale? Alas! **For that Day is great**, **so that none is like it**; **And it is the time of Jacob's** (Israel's) **trouble, but he shall be saved out of it**. 'For it shall come to pass in that Day' says THE LORD of HOSTS, 'That **I will break his** (the enemy's) **yoke from your neck**, and will burst your bonds; **Foreigners shall no more enslave them**, but they shall serve THE LORD their GOD, and David their king, whom I will raise up for them." (JEREMIAH 30:3-9)

"At the 'Time of the End' the King of the South shall attack him; and the **King of the North** shall come against him like a whirlwind, with chariots, horsemen, and with many ships; and he shall enter the Countries, overwhelm them, and pass through. He **shall also enter the Glorious Land**, and many Countries shall be overthrown." (DAN.11:40-41)

According to the Prophetic Portrait outlined in the pages of your Bible, Israel will be invaded and occupied once more. Still, it will receive deliverance from a returning Messiah who will defeat the Beast and his armies in the Battle of Armageddon, and reign over all nations:

> "It shall be in that Day that **I will seek to destroy all the nations that come against Jerusalem**. And I will pour on the House of David and on the inhabitants of Jerusalem the SPIRIT of GRACE and supplication; **then they** (Israel) **will look on Me whom they pierced**. Yes, they will mourn for Him as one mourns for his only son, and grieve for Him as one grieves for a firstborn." (ZECHARIAH 12:9,10 NKJV)

So as you can see, Modern Day Israel is the epicenter of Bible Prophecy - and that's why the recent and current wars in the Middle East are so troubling, as they are events FORETOLD by GOD, which lead up to the Battle of Armageddon and the return of Christ to rule over all nations!

CHAPTER 2

1967 WAR ACQUISITIONS FORETOLD

I was ten years old when the News Media began to report that a major war in the Middle East had broken out. Israel was at war with her Syrian neighbor to the North, Jordanian neighbor to the east, and Egyptian neighbor to the South.

Israeli intelligence had informed the military that war was imminent, so Israel decided on a pre-emptive strike, crippling these three nation's air-forces almost simultaneously. Israeli tanks and infantry also rolled into Gaza and the Sinai Peninsula, quickly taking control of these Egyptian strongholds. The Golan Heights was yanked from Syrian control, and the West Bank of the Jordan River was wrested from Jordanian hands.

In a stunning six days, the war was over – and Israel had acquired lands that it was forecasted to take in Biblical prophecies of old:

"But they (Israel) shall fly down upon the shoulder of the Philistines (Modern-day **Gaza**) toward the West; together they shall plunder the people of the East (Modern-day Jordan); They shall lay their hand on Edom and Moab (**Sinai Peninsula**, **West**

Bank); and the people of Ammon (Amman, Jordan) shall obey them." (ISAIAH 11:14 NKJV)

"The South (of Israel) shall possess the mountains of Esau (**Sinai Peninsula**), and the Lowland (of Israel) shall possess Philistia (**Gaza**), they shall possess the fields of Ephraim and the fields of Samaria (**West Bank**)." (OBADIAH VS. 19 NKJV)

This war could very easily have led to the overthrowing and dissolution of the Israeli State. Instead, the war led to the expansion of Israel's territory, just as these prophecies **FORETOLD**!

The re-planting of Israel as a nation in 1948 and the acquisition of Lands in the 1967 War should have shown the world that **the GOD of the Bible is real** – and that **HE is the best 'Political Forecaster' of future events**!

It also should have made all peoples curious as to what else this PROGNOSTICATOR says about the future. Curious enough to avidly study the Bible and find out for themselves!

CHAPTER 3
CURRENT WAR IN SYRIA FORETOLD

DAMASCUS is one of those rare places on earth that has been continually occupied and has engaged in continuous commerce for 4000 years. True, it has not always been governed by Syrians, but it has never ceased to exist.

So when the Bible **forecasts** the termination of one of the world's oldest cities, people stand up and take notice:

> "A prophecy against DAMASCUS: 'See, **Damascus will no longer be a city but will become a heap of ruins**." (ISAIAH 17:1 NIV)

This pithy prophecy makes a powerful statement that should make every citizen of Damascus shiver with fear and wonderment, in light of the devastation they've witnessed over the last decade's Civil war. But most Syrians are Muslims who are not familiar with such Biblical texts. Even many Christians who are not avid students of the Bible are unaware of this poignant prophecy.

While portions of this ancient city have become a heap of ruins during this war, most of the city is still occupied and still engaging in commerce. But the Syrian Civil War isn't over yet, so this recent destruction in Damascus could be the first step towards the fulfillment of this prophecy.

This precipitous war is still being fought in the northern province of Idlib that shares a border with Turkey to the north and is home to around a thousand ISIS militiamen who have been very difficult to dislodge.

People forget, or are unaware of the fact that the Nation of Turkey cares for some 3.5 million Syrian refugees within its borders. They may also be unaware of the fact that the Turks have entered into an agreement with Russia and Syria (2017) that allowed Turkish weaponry and infantry to enter into Northern Syria to fight ISIS, as well as the Kurds who Ankara labels 'terrorists.'

Syria has since reneged on that agreement, putting Vladimir Putin in a challenging position. Russian support for President Assad is what turned the war around and led to the recovery of Syrian territory from ISIS. But Russia does 25 billion dollars in annual trade with Turkey, while only doing a fraction of that with Syria.

It is easy to see a scenario in which the 3.5 million Syrian Refugees return to Syria one day as Turkish loyalists, who help undermine the Assad Government and aid Turkey into expanding further into Syria. President Erdogan of Turkey has stated publicly that he wants to see the restoration of the Ottoman Empire. Taking over Syria would be the first step in that direction, and we'll have more to say about that in a later chapter.

THE SYRIAN WAR FORETOLD

Meanwhile, there are forecasts about Syria in your Bible that you may not be aware of, yet they've found fulfillment in the Syrian

Civil War of the last decade. Tragically, most Christians are completely unaware of these milestones of Bible Prophecy being fulfilled.

In the 1st year of the Trump Administration, the President launched 59 Tomahawk cruise missiles against the Shayrat Airbase in Syria, three days after the Khan Shaykhun chemical attack that occurred on April 4th, 2017. The President had made it clear to the Assad Government that he would not tolerate the use of chemical weapons as part of the Syrian effort to win the war.

U.S. Intelligence had informed the President that the aircraft used to carry out the chemical attack, which killed 89 people and injured over 500, was based at Shayrat Airbase.

The missile strikes were carried out by Naval Destroyers USS Ross and USS Porter, from the Mediterranean Sea, off the Northwestern Coast of Syria. 58 of the 59 missiles hit their target, and U.S. Secretary of Defense, James Mattis, said that the strike destroyed about 20% of the Syrian Government's operational aircraft and that the Airbase had lost its ability to refuel aircraft.

This mostly forgotten U.S. intervention in the Syrian war went unnoticed as a fulfillment of Biblical prophecy:

> "Against Damascus: '**Hamath & Arpad are shamed**, for they have heard bad news, they are fainthearted; **there is trouble on the Sea**; it cannot be quiet. (JEREMIAH 49:23)

Hamath and Arpad were cities in Ancient Syria, conquered by King Solomon of Israel, who made them storage cities (II CHRONICLES 8:3,4)

If you compare a historic map showing the location of Hamath with a modern-day map of Syria, you'll find it was located in what is the Homs Province today – which is where the Shayrat Airbase is located. 59 Tomahawk missiles striking the base surely made those in the region 'fainthearted,' and it was very 'bad news' for the Assad Regime. The Syrian President surely looked at the U.S. Naval ships off his coast as 'trouble on the Sea.'

The city of Arpaddu has been found on cuneiform inscriptions and is linked to the area of modern-day Aleppo, Syria, which heard its 'bad news' before the Tomahawk strike. Aleppo had seen catastrophic devastation from war from 2012-2016, with an estimated 33,500 buildings either damaged or destroyed.

It's easy to overlook such prophecies, but this is just one more 'milestone' in the Prophetic Portrait outlined in the pages of your Bible, given to sober us spiritually, so that we don't become sleeping virgins (MATTHEW 25:1-13). This parable ends with Christ's admonition:

> "Watch therefore, for you know neither the day nor the hour in which the Son of Man is coming." (MATTHEW 25:13 NKJV)

The prophet Amos also wrote about Damascus, its leaders, and peoples:

> "This is what THE LORD says: 'For three sins of Damascus, even for four, I will not relent. Because she threshed Gilead with sledges having iron teeth, I will send fire on the House of Hazael that will consume the fortresses of Ben-Hadad. I will break down the gate of Damascus; I will destroy the King who is in the Valley of Aven and the one who holds the Scepter in Beth Eden. **The people of Aram** (Syria) **will go into exile to Kir**,' says THE LORD." (AMOS 1:3-5 NIV)

Syria destroyed the Israeli town of Gilead, located east of the Jordan River and north of Jerusalem, under King Hazael in the 9th century B.C. The GOD of Israel promised to return the cruelty with which Syria slew the people of Gilead upon their heads (AMOS 2:13).

Ben-Hadad is a Royal Title used by Syrian kings, meaning, 'Son of Thunder.' It's symbolic of the governing seat of Syria down through the centuries, and this prophecy shows a time in the future in which the one holding the Scepter (rulership) in Syria (currently: Bashar al-Assad) will be destroyed. This will probably happen concurrently with the final destruction of Damascus itself, the prophecy with which we started this chapter (ISAIAH 17:1).

ALMIGHTY GOD often refers to nations in prophecy through their key cities. For example, HE often speaks of Jerusalem when HE's prophesying about Israel, Damascus when HE'S prophesying about Syria. In this prophecy about Syria's future, GOD speaks of the ancient city of 'Kir,' when HE'S speaking of the modern-day nation of Jordan.

The gate of Damascus has been severely damaged over this decade's long war, producing millions of fleeing refugees.

The modern-day areas of Hamath (Homs Province) and Arpad (Aleppo) have 'heard bad news' during the Syrian War, and 1.3 million Syrians have gone into exile to Kir (Jordan).

The odds of all 3 of these events happening in the Modern Age, during the same war - are slim and none! Yet Christians and non-Christians yawned and failed to notice that these prophecies were being fulfilled right under their noses!

Truly, the GOD of the Bible declares "the end from the beginning!" (ISAIAH 46:10 NKJV)

CHAPTER 4
THE RISE & FALL OF 'ISIS' FORETOLD

The World was shocked to see the sudden rise of the **ISLAMIC STATE of IRAQ and SYRIA** (Also known as ISIL – 'the Islamic State of Iraq and the Levant' and 'Daesh'), from the parched sands of these Middle Eastern Nations.

The withdrawal of U.S. troops by the Obama Administration at the end of 2011 created an absence of restraint of radical Sunni forces, seething at the demise of Sunni power that occurred in the toppling of Saddam Hussein's government.

Iraqi born terrorist, Abu Bakr al-Baghdadi, who had 'done time' in the infamous Abu Ghraib Detention Center during the George Bush Jr. war against Iraq, was chosen Caliph of the newly formed Islamic State in June of 2014.

Baghdadi took advantage of the U.S. troop withdrawal, and the Civil War in Syria, which had the Assad Government distracted, to move with German-like Blitzkrieg speed through the sand dunes of Central and Northern Iraq - and the war torn South-Eastern portions of Syria - to seize control of towns and cities in each before these nations knew what hit them!

At the height of its power, ISIS controlled about 40% of Iraq and about 33% of Syria. On June 29th of 2014, Baghdadi formally announced the birth of the Caliphate, stretching from the city of Aleppo near Syria's border with Turkey to the Diyala Province of Central Iraq.

Below are maps of the Ancient Chaldean Empire and the ISIS Caliphate at its height. The native Chaldean territory (highlighted in yellow) on the Chaldean Empire Map of 600 B.C. is a bit larger than the territory ISIS obtained – but occupies much the same areas of Mesopotamia.

The Israeli prophet Habakkuk received his revelation from GOD almost simultaneously with the rise of the Chaldean empire, which he was told in this vision, would rise again suddenly – then quickly fall:

"Look among the nations and watch – **be utterly astounded**! For I (THE LORD) will work a work in your (Heb. 'Yowm' translated 'in that day' 108 times) days which you would not believe, though it were told you. **For indeed I am raising up the Chaldeans**, a bitter and hasty nation which marches through the breadth of the earth, **to possess dwelling places that are not theirs**. They are terrible and dreadful; their judgment and their dignity proceed from themselves. Their horses also are swifter than leopards, and **more fierce than evening wolves**. Their chargers charge ahead; **their cavalry comes from afar**; they fly as the eagle that hastens to eat. They all come for violence; their faces are set like the east wind. They gather captives like sand. **They scoff at kings**, **and princes are scorned by them. They deride every stronghold**, for they heap up earthen mounds and seize it. Then his mind changes and he transgresses; He commits offense **ascribing this power to his god**. (HABAKKUK 1:5-11)

ISIS arose with such speed that the world was **astounded**! And it arose right from within the old Chaldean Empire itself! These terrorists **quickly took possession of dwelling places that were not theirs** and truly **gathered captives like sand**!

Not only were they **more fierce than evening wolves**, they inspired thousands of '**lone wolves**' to commit violent atrocities around the world, killing and maiming people in the public squares of cities, on public transportation, and at sporting events.

More than any army in history, **this Caliphates' cavalry truly came from afar**! According to the New York Times, in September 2014, there were more than 2000 Europeans, 1000 Turks, and 100 Americans fighting for ISIS! By the end of October of the same year, some 2500 Tunisians had joined the ranks of DAESH. A report by the International Centre for Counter-Terrorism – from April 2016 shows that the number of European ISIS recruits had doubled to nearly 4000.

Al-Baghdadi and his supporters **scoffed at world leaders** in regular internet messaging and **seized strategic sites** like the Mosul Dam.

Habakkuk's vision about these modern-day Chaldeans ends with what seems to have led to ISIS' demise: **Ascribing their power and success to their god** (Allah) – when it was the GOD of the Bible (VS.6) that **raised up these offspring of the Chaldeans**, for reasons not given in the text.

What an amazing detailed prophecy - overlooked by the whole world and even most of Christendom! When ISIS came on the world scene, I was doing the nightly news for KFIA radio and told my listeners that the rise of this State was prophesied to occur, through the prophet Habakkuk. Apparently, while all of Humanity struggled to understand and make sense of the shocking rise of ISIS – few people bothered to look and see if the Bible said anything about this momentous event.

THE GREATEST FORECASTER of FUTURE EVENTS said to the prophet Habakkuk:

"Write the vision and make it plain on tablets, that he may RUN who reads it. **For the vision is yet for an appointed time**; but **at the end it will speak**, and it will not lie. Though it tarries, wait for it; Because it will surely come, it will not tarry." (HABAKKUK 2:2,3 NKJV)

This text shows that the visions given to Habakkuk were for an appointed time in the future – not Habakkuk's day. Therefore the rendering of the Hebrew word 'Yowm' in chapter one, verse five as 'your day' is incorrect. **The vision is clearly designated** for '**the end**,' apocalyptic language for the return of Christ and the end of this present Age.

The first part of Habakkuk's vision about a future rise of the Chaldeans (ISIS) has come to pass precisely as prophesied.

What comes next in the vision given to Habakkuk is the rise of a haughty man identical to the Beast like figure we read about in the book of Revelation chapter 13:

"Behold the proud, **his soul is not upright in him**; But the just shall live by his faith. Indeed, because **he transgresses by wine**, he is a proud man, and he does not stay at home. Because he enlarges his desire as hell, and he is like death, and cannot be satisfied **He gathers to himself all nations and heaps up for himself all peoples**. Will not all these take up a proverb against him, and a taunting riddle against him, and say, 'Woe to him who increases what is not his – how long? And to him who loads himself with many pledges'? Will not your creditors rise up suddenly? Will they not awaken who oppress you? And you will become their booty. **Because you have plundered many nations**, all the remnant of the people shall plunder you, be-cause of men's blood and the violence of the land and the city, and of all who dwell in it. (HABAKKUK 2:4-8 NKJV)

More on this individual, and his power and influence in a later chapter.

Take a look at these two maps and compare the Chaldean Empire at its height, with the Islamic State of Iraq and Syria (ISIS) at its height. They are so similar - that it becomes obvious that the prophet Habakkuk was being given a glimpse into the rise of this 'Terrorist State' to come '**at the End**.'

The relevance of the Bible to 'our day and age' is magnified in visions like this, that clearly show that 'the rise and fall of ISIS' was DIVINELY **FORETOLD**!

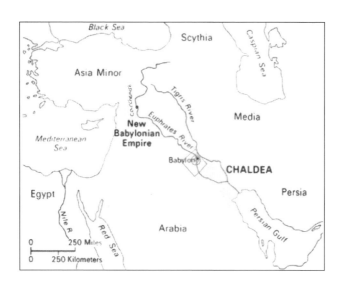

CHAPTER 5
THE 'COVID 19' EFFECT

Just as the opening chapter of HABAKKUK started out with a prophecy fulfilled in the present day (The rise & fall of ISIS), so too, the book of ZECHARIAH begins with a prophecy the world has just experienced, but was not aware of:

"On the 24th Day of the 11th month, which is the month Shebat (**FEB.19TH, 2020 according to the Jewish/Hebrew Date Converter - Chabad.org**), in the 2nd year of Darius, the word of THE LORD came to Zechariah son of Berechiah, the son of Iddo the prophet: 'I saw by night, and behold, a man riding on a red horse, and it stood among the myrtle trees in the hollow; and behind him were horses: red, sorrel, and white. Then I said, 'My Lord, what are these?' So the Angel who talked with me said to me, 'I will show you what they are.' And the man who stood among the myrtle trees answered and said, 'These are the ones whom THE LORD has sent to walk to and fro throughout the earth.' So they answered the Angel of THE LORD, who stood among the myrtle trees, and said, 'We have walked to and fro throughout the earth, and behold, **all the earth is resting quietly**." (ZECHARIAH 1:7-11 NKJV)

I've wondered for years about **what could possibly happen at the same time all over the world to make all the earth rest quietly - as this prophecy FORETOLD?** And then as I watched the news, as everyone did from the middle of February to the end of May, and saw the whole world shuts down its streets and businesses because of the COVID 19 PANDEMIC, and listened to the eerie silence come over the land – I thought '**This prophecy is being fulfilled right before our eyes and ears!**' Stadiums, Malls, Public Parks, Public Beaches, Commercial and Government buildings – all void of people. The roar of freeways, the vibration of machinery, the reverberation of music, the cheers of crowds, the honking of horns, the shrill sound of sirens – virtually all silenced! And not in just one city, or county, but across the country and around the world! And for the better part of 2 whole months!

Sound's loudness is measured in decibels: Normal conversation registers around 60 decibels of volume; Office conversation, 70 decibels; Lawn-mowers and heavy traffic hover around 90 decibels; chain-saws, leaf-blowers, sports crowds, and rock music concerts come in at about 120 decibels. Any noise over 85 decibels is damaging to human hearing.

It's impossible to put a number on Human Civilization's combined 'decibel generation' in 'normal busy times' – but the fact that it was reduced to a small fraction of what it was before 'the shutdown' – all around the world at once – is truly without parallel!

In a recent article entitled: 'Why everything is getting louder,' author, Bianca Bosker, wrote:

"Though data are scarce, the world appears to be growing louder. The National Park Service's Natural Sounds and Night Skies Division, which sends researchers to measure the acoustics of the American outdoors, estimates that noise pollution doubles or triples every 30 years. The EPA last measured our nation's volume in 1981; assuming (generously) that our collective cacophony has remained constant, calculations from 2013 estimate that more than 145 million Americans are exposed to noise exceeding the recommended limits." (The Atlantic, 'Why Everything is Getting Louder' November 2019 Issue)

While this reprieve from damaging noise levels is welcome, the 'Shelter in place' orders from our Local, State, and Federal Governments, have put a tremendous strain on other aspects of Human Health.

What are the odds that a disease labeled with the number '19' (the year it began 2019) would cause **the whole world to rest quietly** – through a prophecy given 2500 years ago on the 19th day of the month (February) – the same time of year that this pestilence began to spread throughout the world?

And how improbable is it that most of the World's National Leaders would give the same 'Shelter in place' order, at the same time, over the same disease epidemic, to bring about this effect?

On June 11th, 2009, the World Health Organization (WHO) declared the Swine Flu Outbreak a pandemic – yet world leaders did not give a 'Shelter in place' order.

Ditto that with the previous Disease Pandemics going back over a century to the Spanish Flu Outbreak of 1918-1920, which killed somewhere between 20-50 million people!

Whether it was a matter of World Leaders 'following the herd', or being overly cautious, we've never seen an orchestrated shut-down of this magnitude in Human History!

A 2ND REST

Your Bible only mentions **the whole world being at rest TWICE**! The 2nd incidence is easy to understand as it describes the state of the world immediately after the Battle of Armageddon:

> "Take up this proverb against the King of Babylon and say: '**How the Oppressor** (Beast) **has ceased**! THE LORD has broken the staff of the wicked, the Scepter of the Rulers; He who struck the people in wrath with a continual stroke, **he who ruled the nations in anger**, **is persecuted and no one hinders**. **The whole earth is at rest and quiet**; They break forth into singing. Indeed the cypress trees rejoice over you, and the cedars of Lebanon, saying, '**Since you were cut down**, **no woodsman has come up against us.**' Hell from beneath is excited about you, to meet you at your coming; It stirs up the dead for you, all the chief ones of the earth; It has raised up from their thrones all the kings of the nations. They all shall speak and say to you: 'Have you also become as weak as we? Have you become like us? Your pomp is brought down to Sheol (the grave), and the sound of your stringed instruments; the maggot is spread under you, and worms cover you.' (ISAIAH 14:4-11 NKJV)

That will be a gloriously quiet time, for parallel with it will be the reign of Christ over all nations from Jerusalem (REV.11:15)! And under His reign, peace will cover the earth:

"He (Jesus) shall judge between the nations, and rebuke many people; They shall beat their swords into plowshares, and their spears into pruning hooks; **Nation shall not lift up sword against nation**, **neither shall they learn war anymore**." (ISAIAH 2:4)

We've all seen, either in pictures or in person, the bronze statue in the gardens beside the United Nations building – donated by the Soviet Union – with the inscription 'Let us beat swords into Ploughshares,' taken from this text of Scripture. What this Human Organization has utterly failed to bring about (there have been hundreds of wars fought since its founding) – Christ will make a reality – and **the whole world will be at rest for a thousand years** (REV.20:4)

BACK TO THE '1st REST'

Let's return to the discussion of the **COVID 19 VIRUS** that moved world leaders to shut down the earth's bustling economy and social activities - effecting this 1st Biblical fulfillment of **the earth resting quietly**.

This Health Crisis has caused people throughout the world to ask, '**Why does GOD allow Disease Pandemics? Why did GOD create bacteria and viruses in the first place?** And **why would HE allow them to spread through Christian Countries?**

Two parallel chapters in your Bible (LEVITCUS 26 & DEUTERONOMY 28), often called 'The Blessings and Cursing Chapters,' give us the answers to these questions. In them, GOD says that if Israel walked according to HIS word, it would be blessed in the City, the fields, the weather, and the womb. But if they refused, and walked in rebellion to GOD'S word, then they as a people would be cursed with among other things, "**wasting disease and fever which shall consume the eyes and cause sorrow of heart…I will send pestilence** (Virulent Disease) **among you…**" (LEVITICUS 26:16,25 NKJV)

The 21st Century has seen three major viral outbreaks in the world, SARS, MERS & COVID 19! And GOD shows in other texts that these 'Blessings and Cursing' are not just applied to Israel – but to all nations:

"…When a land sins against ME by persistent unfaithfulness, **I will stretch out MY HAND against it**; I will cut off its supply of bread, send famine on it, and cut off man and beast from it." (EZEKIEL 14:13 NKJV)

"The prophets who have been before me and before you of old prophesied against **many countries and great kingdoms**, of war and disaster and **pestilence**." (JEREMIAH 28:8)

But GOD in HIS BENEVOLENCE tells us how to avoid the plague of pestilence from coming upon our nation:

"If you diligently heed the voice of THE LORD your GOD and do what is right in HIS SIGHT, give ear to HIS commandments and keep all HIS statutes, **I will put none of these diseases on you** which I have brought on the Egyptians. **For I AM THE LORD WHO HEALS you**." (EXODUS 15:26 NKJV)

DISEASE is clearly something which people and nations can avoid – if they let GOD'S word rule their lives! But if not, our CREATOR clearly states that DISEASE will run rampant in our Societies!

Our CREATOR even showed the world how to contain disease when it strikes:

"…Then the priest shall **ISOLATE** the one who has the sore 7 days… Now the leper on whom the sore is… shall dwell alone; **his dwelling shall be outside the camp**." (LEVITICUS 13:4,45,46 NKJV)

This is the oldest historical record of the invocation of QUARANTINE – and it didn't come through the Scientific Method or Philosophical reasoning – but through revelation from GOD! Yet every time it's invoked by cities or nations - no credit is given to THE SOURCE of the practice!

The word 'Quarantine' comes from the Venetian term 'Quranta Giorni' meaning '40 days' and refers to the period of time that all ships arriving in Venice had to wait offshore during the Black Plague. Ironically, the Nation that coined the term QUARANTINE was the First Nation outside of China to invoke the act of isolating all its citizens in a 'stay at home order,' during the recent COVID 19 PANDEMIC.

According to the World Health Organization (WHO), chronic diseases are the leading cause of death worldwide – yet it's all so unnecessary and avoidable – if we would simply acquiesce to THE CREATOR'S WILL instead of our own!

What is the significance of COVID-19 effecting the most peaceful two months in Human History, causing **all the earth to rest quietly**? Well, according to the rest of the book of Zechariah, in which this is the first recorded prophetic event, **this is 'THE CALM BEFORE the STORM' of 'End Time' Events, Leading up to the Return of Jesus Christ, the Battle of Armageddon, and**

the setting up of Christ's rule over all nations for a 1000 years (REVELATION 20:6)

What does GOD say will happen next through the prophet Zechariah? Read the rest of the first chapter of Zechariah and find out!

CHAPTER 6
ZECHARIAH'S 2ND VISION - '4 HORNS'

If you read on into the 1st chapter of the book of Zechariah after the Angels report to GOD that **all the earth is resting quietly,** you'll read the 2nd of 8 Visions given to the prophet:

> "**Then I raised my eyes and looked, and there were 4 Horns**. And I said to the Angel who talked with me, 'What are these?' So he answered me, '**These are the Horns that have scattered Judah, Israel, and Jerusalem**.' Then THE LORD showed me 4 Craftsmen. And I said, 'What are these coming to do?' So he said, 'These are the Horns that scattered Judah, so that no one could lift up his head; but **the Craftsmen are coming to terrify them, to cast out the Horns of the nations that lifted up their Horn against the Land of Judah to scatter it**." (ZECHARIAH 1:18-21 NKJV)

Where else do we read about 4 Horns in your Bible? Only one place, the 7th chapter of the book of Daniel:

> "After this I (Daniel) saw in the night visions, and behold, a 4th Beast, dreadful and terrible, exceedingly strong. It had huge

iron teeth; it was devouring, breaking in pieces and trampling the residue with its feet. It was different from all the Beasts that were before it, and it had 10 Horns. I was considering the Horns, and **there was another Horn, a little one,** coming up among them, **before whom 3 of the first Horns were plucked out by the roots** (3 + 1 = 4 Horns). And there in **this Horn,** were eyes like the eyes of a man and a mouth speaking pompous words." (DANIEL 7:7,8 NKJV)

"**Then I** (Daniel) **wished to know the truth about the 4th Beast**…And the 10 Horns that were on its (4th Beast's) head, and **the other Horn which came up, before which 3 fell** (3 + 1 = 4), namely, **that Horn** which had eyes and a mouth which spoke pompous words, **whose appearance was greater than his fellows**." (DANIEL 7:19,20 NKJV)

The 10 Horns are 10 Kings who shall arise from this kingdom (4th Beast). **And another shall rise after them**; He shall be different from the first ones and **shall subdue 3 kings** (3 + 1 = 4). He shall speak pompous words against THE MOST HIGH (As does the Beast, Rev.13:5) persecute the Saints of THE MOST HIGH (As does the Beast, Rev.13:7) and shall intend to change Times and Law. Then the Saints shall be given into his hand for a time, times, and half a time (3 ½ years same as under the Beast, Rev.13:50)." (DANIEL 7:24,25)

Three times, no doubt for emphasis, GOD ALMIGHTY shows us the 'three plus one' formula that results in the 4 Horns of Zechariah's prophecy. The plucking up or subduing of 3 of the 10 kings represented by 10 Horns on the 4th Beast, seems to be a separate event that is a precursor to the 10 Horns 'giving their power and authority to the Beast' (REVELATION 17:12,13).

And then in chapter 8 of the book of Daniel, we find this 'Little Horn' troubling Israel:

> Therefore the Male Goat (Greece Dan.8:21) grew very great; but when he became strong, the large Horn (History says: Alexander the Great) was broken, and in place of it four notable ones came up toward the 4 winds of heaven (History says: **4 Generals of Alexander**). **And out of one of them** (not the European Union or Russia), **came a** '**Little Horn**' which grew exceedingly great toward the South, toward the East, and toward the Glorious Land (Israel)… He even exalted himself as high as the Prince of the Host (II Thes.2:3,4); and by him the daily sacrifices were taken away..." (DANIEL 8:8-11 NKJV)

Do a study of 'Horns' in your Bible, and you'll see that it is a symbol of kings, kingdoms, and National or Empirical might (I SAMUEL 2:10) (JEREMIAH 48:25).

This text in the 8th Chapter of Daniel reveals the 'Little Horn' comes out of the Northern Division of Alexander's Empire (since it grows exceedingly great toward the South, East, and the Glorious Land of Israel, Southwest – it must be coming from the north). History records this to be the Seleucid Empire of General Seleucus I Nicator, which stretched from Asia Minor through the Levant and would include modern-day Syria, Iran, Iraq, and parts of Afghanistan. It is clearly from out of this geographical region that the future 'Little Horn' comes.

The expansion of the 'Little Horn' in Daniel's Vision **refers to the time of the end** (8:17). Therefore, his rise to power and plucking up and subduing of 3 other Horns has yet to occur.

Here's a Biblical 'prophetic sketch' of the kind of personality and stature this **end-time 'Little Horn'** will have:

"As for the broken horn (Alexander) and the 4 that stood up in its place, 4 kingdoms shall arise out of that nation, but not with its power. And in the 'latter time' of their kingdom, when the transgressors have reached their fullness, **a king shall arise, having fierce features**, who understands sinister schemes. **His power shall be mighty, but not by his own power; He shall destroy fearfully, and shall prosper and thrive; He shall destroy the mighty, and also the holy people** (Israel). **Through his cunning he shall cause deceit to prosper under his rule**; And **he shall exalt himself in his heart. He shall destroy many in their prosperity. He shall even rise against the Prince of Princes** (Jesus Christ); **But he shall be broken without Human means**." (DANIEL 8:22-25 NKJV)

What a dark description of a Rogue Dictator! But notice that this 'Little Horn's' power is not his own – just as the real power behind the throne of the coming 'Beast' is not his own – but "**the dragon** (Satan) **gave him his power, his throne, and great authority**." (REVELATION 13:2) Therefore the 'Little Horn' and 'the Beast' are the same person, an 'end time' leader of a kingdom that will destroy 'the mighty' (The U.S., Russia, China?) and Israel – empowered by Satan! Cunning and deceit will help him prosper – which is what you would expect from a leader who "**confirms a covenant with many**" (DANIEL 9:27) – and then breaks it!

A TALE of 4 CITIES

Most people have heard of, or read, Charles Dickens Historical Novel: 'A TALE of 2 CITIES' – (London and Paris) – telling of life during the infamous REIGN of TERROR that led to the French Revolution in the late 18th century.

Well, your Bible tells 'A Tale of 4 Cities,' all located in the same modern-day nation prophesied to be the center of the final world-ruling empire called THE BEAST in Revelation chapter 13.

The first City we'll discuss is Antioch (where followers of Christ were first called Christians ACTS 11:26). This ancient city was built by Seleucus I Nicator, whose kingdom was the northern division of Alexander's Empire, out of which will arise the 'Little Horn.' It still exists today and is located in what is now South-Eastern Turkey.

Upon Alexander's death, his vast kingdom was divided among 4 of his generals, who warred against one another in finally establishing their territories. In the most detailed prophecy in all the Bible, Daniel was told by an angel about the future division of Alexander the Great's empire:

> "Now then, I (an Angel) tell you (Daniel) the truth: 3 more kings will arise in Persia and then a 4th, who will be far richer than all the others. When he has gained power by his wealth, he will stir up everyone against the Kingdom of Greece. Then a mighty King will arise (Alexander), who will rule with great power and do as he pleases. After he has arisen, his empire will be broken up and parceled out toward the 4 winds of heaven (north, south, east, and west). It will not go out to his descendants (none of Alexander's generals were kin), nor will it have the power he exercised, because his empire will be uprooted and given to others (his generals). (DANIEL 11:2-4 NIV)

The city of Antioch was located Northeast of Egypt, thus the Angel's designation of general (Seleucus) who founded it, as THE

KING of THE NORTH. Antioch remained the capital of the Seleucid Kingdom for the next two centuries and became an identifying sign of THE FINAL KING of THE NORTH (Turkey) at THE TIME of THE END (DANIEL 11:40)

There is no exegetical reason to teach that at 'the time of the end,' described in Daniel 11:40-45 – the Kings of the North and South represent new nations or kingdoms. Yet that is exactly what advocates of a European or Russian Beast maintain, without any basis for doing so.

The Bible's TALE of 4 CITIES continues in the message given to the Church at **Pergamos** by Jesus:

> "To the Angel of the Church in **Pergamum** write: 'These are the words of Him (Jesus) who has the sharp, double-edged sword. I know where you live - **WHERE SATAN HAS HIS THRONE**. Yet you remain true to My name. You did not renounce your faith in Me, not even in the days of Antipas, My faithful witness, who was put to death in your city – **WHERE SATAN LIVES**." (REVELATION 2:13 NIV)

Pergamum is now modern-day Bergama, Turkey. Remember that the book of Revelation is a prophetic book: "...**to show HIS servants what must soon take place**." (REVELATION 1:1 NIV) Jesus tells us twice for emphasis **where Satan's throne is**. Also remember that **it is the Dragon that gives THE BEAST**: "...**His power and His throne and great authority**." (REVELATION 13:2 NIV) How easy it is to overlook such insightful statements! I did it for years, reading right over the significance of a statement made by our Messiah meant to show us the earthly headquarters of the 'god of this world' (II CORINTHIANS 4:4), who according to Christ has also 'deceived the whole world' (REVELATION 12:9)!

Two more of the Bible's TALE of 4 CITIES are **Meshech** and **Tubal**, which according to Josephu**s**, and Eusebius, **were two Cities in Eastern Asia Minor** (Modern day Turkey). Concerning these Cities, we read in Wikipedia:

> "Modern Scholarship has identified the Biblical **Tubal** with Tabal, an Anatolian (Turkish) state and region mentioned in Assyrian sources. Tabal was a post-Hittite Luwian State in Asia Minor in the first Millenium B.C. Its neighbors, the Mushki, are traditionally associated with **Meshech**. Some historians further connect Tabal and Tubal with the tribe on the Black Sea coast later known to the Greeks as Tibareni, though this identification is uncertain. Most reference books, following Flavius Josephus, identify **Tubal** in Ezekiel's time as an area that is now in **Turkey**."

Meshech and Tubal are first mentioned in THE TABLE OF NATIONS found in the book of GENESIS, as sons of Japheth. They are almost always mentioned together:

> "The sons of Japheth were Gomer, Magog, Madai, Javan, Tubal, **Meshech** and Tiras." (GENESIS 10:2)

> "Javan, **Tubal**, and **Meshech** were your (Tyre's) traders. They bartered human lives (slavery) and vessels of bronze for your merchandise." (EZEKIEL 27:13)

Meshech and Tubal are not eponyms for Moscow and Tobolsk, 2 cities in Russia, which many prophecy enthusiasts have errantly equated with these Biblical names. According to Ezekiel, they were two ancient city/states known in Ezekiel's day as trading partners with the port city of Tyre, directly north across the Mediterranean Sea.

They are most famously connected to a prince who stirs up many peoples against Israel in the latter times:

"The word of THE LORD came to me (Ezekiel): Son of man, set your face against Gog, of the land of Magog, **the chief prince of Meshech and Tubal**; prophesy against **him** and say: 'This is what THE SOVEREIGN LORD says: I am against you, **Gog, chief prince of Meshech and Tubal**. I will turn you around, put hooks in your jaws and bring you out with your whole army – your horses, your horsemen fully armed, and a great horde with large and small shields, all of them brandishing their swords. Persia (Modern Day Iran), Cush (Modern Day Sudan), and Put (Modern Day Libya) will be with them, all with shields and helmets, also Gomer (Western Asia Minor) with all its troops, and Beth Togarmah from the far north with all its troops – the many nations with you. Get ready; be prepared, you and all the hordes gathered about you and take command of them. After many days you will be called to arms. In future years you will invade a land that has recovered from war, whose people were gathered from many nations to the mountains of Israel, which had long been desolate… **This is what will happen in THAT DAY**: When Gog attacks the land of Israel, MY HOT ANGER will be aroused, declares THE SOVEREIGN LORD. In MY zeal and fiery wrath I declare **at that time there shall be A GREAT EARTHQUAKE in the land of Israel** (parallel: Rev.16:18) … On that day I will give Gog a burial place in Israel, in the valley of those who travel east of the Sea… **Call out to every kind of bird and all the wild animals**: Assemble and come together from all around to **the sacrifice** I am preparing for you, the great sacrifice on the mountains of Israel. There you will eat flesh and drink blood. You will eat the flesh of mighty men and drink the blood of the princes of the earth…" (EZEKIEL 38:1-8; 18,19; 2:11,17,18) (parallel: REV.19:17,18).

The annals of the Assyrian King, Ashurbanipal (668 - 627 B.C.), refer several times to **Gugu**, King of Luddi, (Lydia, western Asia Minor, modern-day Turkey). Ezekiel wrote about Gog around 50 years later (593-571 B.C.), when the exploits of this King would have been well known by all Mediterranean nations.

This ancient figure Gog, spoken of prophetically and linked to 'That Day' and 'The Latter Years' **is a forerunner of an end-time leader who unites peoples who are all Muslim today**!

Gog (EZEKIEL 38:18), **the King of the North** (DANIEL 11:41), **The Beast** (REVELATION 11:1-7), and the '**Little Horn**' (DANIEL 8:9), are all prophesied to invade the Nation of Israel at '**the time of the End**' – leading many to believe they are merely different titles for the same diabolical leader!

The Bible's TALE of 4 CITIES: **Pergamum** (where Satan's throne is), **Antioch** (Head-quarters of the King of the North), **Meshech, and Tubal** (where Gog is the Chief Prince) – is meant to identify to readers – **THAT TURKEY WILL BE THE KEY NATION TO WATCH in THE END TIMES**, the residence of both the Devil and His puppet 'The Beast!'

Turkey ranks 11th on the GLOBAL FIREPOWER INDEX, which ranks the 'military might' of nations. It has the 14th largest standing army and the 18th largest economy. This 'Little Horn' can be made mightier than all other nations, however, through Satan's empowerment! And when she takes over all the Middle East as she is prophesied to do (DANIEL 11:40-45) – Turkey would have control of the 2/3 of the world's oil, 400 million citizens, and the combined military might of dozens of nations!

Turkey's President Erdogan has stated publicly that he wants to restore the Ottoman Empire, which would bring the Middle Eastern Nations under his reign.

Remember that **THE BEAST** with HIS 10 KINGS eventually turns on **THE GREAT HARLOT CITY** and burns HER with fire (REVELATION 17:16). The Prophet Jeremiah was inspired to tell us what peoples would accomplish this destruction of **BABYLON, THE GREAT HARLOT**:

> "Set up a banner in the Land, blow the trumpet among the nations! Prepare the nations against HER (Babylon), call the kingdoms together against HER: **Ararat** (Turkey), Minni (Persia), and Ashkenaz (Kazakhstan, Turkmenistan, Tajikistan). Appoint a general (**Gog**) against HER; cause the horses to come up like the bristling locusts. Prepare against HER the nations, with the kings of the Medes (Southern Iran), its governors and all its rulers, all the land of his (Gog's) dominion. And the land will tremble and sorrow; for every purpose of THE LORD shall be performed against Babylon, to make the land of Babylon a desolation without inhabitant." (JER.51:2729)

The Prophetic Portrait outlined in the pages of your Bible revolves around the modern-day nation of Turkey!

CHAPTER 7

COMING WAR AGAINST IRAN FORETOLD

If I was a prophet talking about what's going to happen to Californians, Texans, Georgians, and New Yorkers 2500 years from now – you would know that I was prophesying about the United States of America… because our Nation is made up of these and many other people states.

So when GOD ALMIGHTY told us 2500 years ago what's going to happen to **Parthian**s, **Persian**s, **Medes, and Elamites in our day** – Christians should know that their Bible is speaking of modern-day **Iran**!

The events of 2019: the **attack against the American Embassy in Iraq**, **the assassination of** the leading Iranian Guard Military strategist, **Soleimani**, and **Iran's retribution in the form of a missile attack against Iraqi bases with U.S. Personnel** – has a lot of prophecy experts thinking this may be the lead up to the fulfillment of Jeremiah's prophecy about the destruction of Iran!

Until 1935 Iran was known to the world as Persia. Persia was an exonym – a name given to a people by outside nations, but the people of that nation have always referred to themselves as Irani.

So in 1935, the government there informed the world that the Irani people wanted to be referred to as 'Iran.'

Modern Day **Iran** is made up of peoples referred to in your Bible as **Medes** (northern Iran), **Persians** (Southern Iran), **Elam** (western Iran), and **Parthia** (eastern Iran). We find 3 of these peoples mentioned together in the book of ACTS:

"When the Day of Pentecost came, they (the disciples) were all together in one place. Suddenly a sound like the blowing of a violent wind came from heaven and filled the whole house where they were sitting… All of them were filled with THE HOLY SPIRIT and began to speak in other tongues as THE SPIRIT enabled them. Now there were staying in Jerusalem GOD-fearing Jews from every nation under heaven… **Parthians, Medes, and Elamites**…" (ACTS 2:1,2,4,5,9)

It was a Persian King (Cyrus) that THE LORD moved to make a decree to let the people of Israel return and rebuild Jerusalem and the temple. (ISAIAH 44:28; 45:1) (II CHRONICLES 36:22,23) (EZRA 1:1-4)

Ironically, a later Persian King (Xerxes/Ahasuerus) signed a decree to annihilate the Jewish people! He signed the decree at the urging of Haman, whose father was an Agagite (ESTHER 3:8-14 - people who have an ancient hatred of Israelites). Ironically, the name Khomeini (pronounced 'Homani') shares Semitic roots with the name Haman! History tells us that Haman, Herod, Hitler, and 'Homani' have all called for or attempted Genocide against the Israeli people!

Is it just a coincidence that the modern-day leaders of Iran have also been calling for the destruction of Israel? Former President of Iran (Mahmoud Ahmadinejad) was known for his inflammatory and provocative language regarding the modern State of Israel. And the Imams of Iran, who are the real power behind the throne, have also made existential threats against the Jewish people.

A future Confederacy of Middle Eastern Nations will also make taunting threats against **Israel**, saying, "Come, and **let us cut them off from being a nation**." (PSALM 83:4)

In the GLOBAL FIRE-POWER RANKING of 'Nations Military Might' – Iran is ranked #14. Iran is often referred to in the news as '**The Chief State Sponsor of Terror**,' meaning that it's a Country that openly funds and facilitates terrorist acts in other nations - unlike Al-Qaeda, Boko Haram, and ISIS, which are roaming, 'Stateless' conductors of terror.

Most people aren't aware of the fact that Iran is the foremost of **Shi'a Islam might**. Shi'a Islam was formed out of a desire to see the successor to Muhammad be a relative (**Monarchy**), where Sunni Islam arose from the desire to see the most qualified person succeed him (**Meritocracy**).

After the fall of Saddam Hussein and his Sunni government, Shi'a leaders became the dominant force in power, which in part responsible for the rise of the Sunni ISIS State. Iran also helped the Assad government of Syria to defeat ISIS, so the Syrian government is indebted to Iran.

Most are also unaware that Shi'a Iran is completely surrounded by Sunni predominant Nations to the north, south, east and west of her. **Here's a map showing Shi'a Iran encircled by Sunni Islam**:

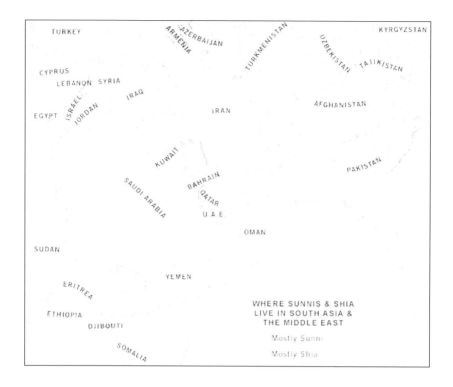

With this Sunni-Shi'a Divide in mind – consider this 2500-year-old prophecy about the fate of **Elam**, which any Bible Dictionary will verify is modern-day **Iran**:

> "The word of THE LORD that came to Jeremiah the prophet against **Elam**, in the beginning of the reign of Zedekiah, King of Judah, saying, Thus says THE LORD of HOSTS, 'Behold, **I will break the bow of Elam**, **the foremost of their** (Shi'a) **might. Against Elam I will bring the 4 winds from the 4 quarters of heaven** (Nations from all 4 sides) and scatter them towards all these winds; There shall be no nations where the outcasts of **Elam** will not go. For I will cause Elam to be dismayed before

their enemies and before those who seek their life. **I will bring disaster upon them**, MY fierce anger says THE LORD; And I will send the sword after them until I have consumed them. **I will set MY throne in Elam**, and will destroy from there the King and the Princes…" (JEREMIAH 49:34-38 NKJV)

Back in December of 2015, Saudi Arabia formed a 34 Country Coalition of Sunni Nations to deal with the Iranian terrorist and nuclear threat. These nations are made up of the Sunni nations you see in the map above, along with some African nations not shown.

Because modern-day Israel is also greatly concerned about Iran's nuclear program, its taunting threats to wipe them off the map, and its military support of Hezbollah and Hamas – the Israeli government has been in 'not so secret talks' with the Saudi's and other Sunni neighbors about how to minimize the 'Persian Problem.'

These 34 Sunni Nations, along with the aid of Israel, could very quickly fulfill Jeremiah's prophecy, attacking Iran from all four directions! Your Bible doesn't tell us what the catalyst for this war will be. Still, Israel has let it be known that they are watching Iran's nuclear development, and will not allow them to reach a certain threshold that would enable them to create 'dirty' bombs – let alone a fully operative nuclear warhead. We may wake up one morning to the news that this war has begun!

Once the onslaught begins against Iran, the '**Little Horn**' attacking **from the north, may see this as his opportunity to 'pluck up' and 'subdue' 3 Horns** (Syria, Iraq, and Iran)! **Turkey** already has tens of thousands of troops inside the northern Syrian and Iraqi borders because of the on-going war there against the remnants of ISIS and the Kurds whom they see as a centuries-old enemy.

Turkey's subjugation of these 3 nations also MUST happen in order for the 'King of the North' to be restored to its power and geographical dominion it had in the post-Alexandrian era -prophesied in the 11th chapter of DANIEL.

The devastating war against Iran is poised to happen, and the 'Little Horn' is ready and wanting to become the 'King of the North' once again! **Both prophecies may very well be fulfilled simultaneously!**

Below is a map of the former Seleucid Kingdom of the 'King of the North', showing that the territory Turkey would have to 'pluck up' includes modern-day Syria, Iraq, and Iran.

CHAPTER 8
THE CAUSE OF 'TERROR'

It may surprise you to know that the word '**TERROR**' occurs over 50 times in your Bible! The Hebrew word 'Behalah' is translated **Panic**, **Destruction**, **Terror,** and **Trouble** in English.

What is the cause of 'Terror' coming upon a nation according to your Bible? The answer is found in the third book of Scripture:

"**But if you do not obey ME**, and do not observe all these commandments… I also will do this to you: **I will even appoint TERROR over you**… I will set MY FACE against you, and you shall be defeated by your enemies. Those who hate you shall reign over you, and you shall flee when no one pursues you." (LEVITICUS 26:14,16,17 NKJV)

The reason the western nations of Europe and the Americas have been **TERRORIZED** the last two decades, is because we have departed from our Judeo-Christian roots that brought blessings from GOD upon our nations. If you take the time to read the first 13 verses of this same chapter, you'll find that our CREATOR promises to bless us with peace and prosperity – if we walk according to HIS word and instructions. The Christian Nations of 'the West' used to take such promises seriously, and it showed in national blessing! But the last half-century has seen the supplanting of Judeo-Christian Ethics with Liberal Ethics – and a remarkable decline in morality – so GOD has appointed **TERROR** over us!

ALMIGHTY GOD says:

"Because I have called and you refused, I have stretched out MY HAND (to lead) and no one regarded, because you disdained all MY COUNSEL, and would have none of MY REBUKE, I also will laugh at your calamity; **I will mock when your TERROR comes, when your TERROR comes like a storm**, and your destruction comes like a whirlwind, when distress and anguish come upon you. Then they will call on ME, but I will not answer; They will seek ME diligently, but they will not find ME. **Because they hated knowledge** and did not choose the fear of THE LORD, they would have none of MY COUNSEL and despised MY EVERY REBUKE. Therefore they shall eat the fruit of their own way, and be filled to the full with their own fancies." (PROVERBS 1:24-31 NKJV)

When this nation was TERRORIZED on 9-11 – people flocked back to the Churches throughout America to call upon THE LORD in prayer and humility. But our repentance was shallow and short-lived, and soon we returned to 'sin as usual' – forgetting GOD'S REBUKE!

Back in the introduction of this book, I talked about the fact that there are three sources of knowledge The Scientific method, the Human reasoning and reflection of Philosophy, and Revelation from GOD. **Because we have come to HATE this 3rd branch of KNOWLEDGE in 'the West'** – **TERROR continues to be**

appointed over us - And not just TERROR but 'Wasting Disease' (Like COVID-19) as the second punishment listed to come upon immoral nations (LEVITICUS 26:16)!

The book of Proverbs also tells us: "It is a joy for the just to do justice, **but DESTRUCTION will come to the workers of iniquity.**" (PROVERBS 21:15 NKJV)

Ironically, the Bible chapter that contains the word 'TERROR' the most is one of the most overlooked prophecies in your Bible! It identifies what nations have been **CAUSING TERROR** in these days leading up to the return of CHRIST when He will recompense that **TERROR** upon their heads.

This chapter is written as a postscript looking back at the aftermath of the Battle of Armageddon when millions of men's bodies have been buried in the graves:

"Assyria (Modern day **SYRIA & IRAQ**) is there (Megiddo) with her whole army; she is surrounded by the graves of all her slain... All **who had spread TERROR** in the land of the living... Elam (Modern day **IRAN**) is there, with all her hordes around her grave... **Because their TERROR had spread** in the land of the living... Meshek and Tubal (Modern day **TURKEY**) are there... **because they spread their TERROR** in the land of the living.,. Edom (Modern day **JORDAN**)... All the princes of the North and all the Sidonians (Modern day **LEBANNON**) are there... they went down with the slain in disgrace despite **the TERROR caused by their power**... Pharaoh (**EGYPT**) – he and all his army... **although I (THE LORD) had him spread TERROR** in the land of the living." (EZEKIEL 32:22-32 NIV)

These are all Muslim peoples today, which is the source of Radical Islam and their TERRORIST ACTS felt round the world! Many of these same peoples are mentioned by Ezekiel again in chapters 38 and 39 – as **those led by Gog to the battle of Armageddon**! How did Ezekiel know which peoples in the future would be causing TERROR in our day and age!

If such a detailed and accurate list of nations perpetrating **TERROR** on the earth in our day and age were found in any other book besides the Bible, it would have made front-page news in nations around the world!

If every pulpit in America, the weekend after 9-11, had covered what the Bible says about **TERROR** and its causes, along with what nations would be the perpetrators of such **TERROR** according to Bible prophecy – Christians would have been astounded at what they heard. They would have seen how relevant the Bible is to our day and age - and our repentance as a nation would have been more genuine and far-reaching!

But instead – we tread ahead – oblivious to how many Biblical prophecies are being fulfilled in the headlines we read, and how actively involved our CREATOR is in what is happening in the world today!

HE warned us that TERROR and WASTING DISEASE would be the first two CURSES HE would bring upon disobedient nations – and HE'S done just that! Throughout the Bible, we read how GOD allowed other nations to punish Israel and then turned around and retaliated against those nations for their sins!

How do we escape such TERROR as nations and individuals? Here's how:

"**But whoever listens to ME will dwell safely**, and will be secure, without fear of evil." (PROVERBS 1:32 NKJV)

"**Do not be afraid of SUDDEN TERROR**, nor of trouble from the wicked when it comes; for THE LORD will be your confidence, and will keep your foot from being caught." (PROVERBS 3:25 NKJV)

CHAPTER 9
ARAB 'RECOGNITION' OF ISRAEL

What will the map of the Middle East look like after the war against Iran has been fought? If Turkey takes advantage of the situation and 'plucks up' and subdues 3 Horns (Syria, Iraq & Iran), then those nations will be annexed by the Ottomans and no longer appear on maps of the region!

But another consequence of this war will be that Sunni nations will be indebted to Israel for their help against Iran, and will be much more likely to officially recognize the Israeli state for the first time in her modern replanting as a nation.

If Israel aids the Sunni Coalition in taking out the nuclear program of Iran, and in ultimately bringing down the Shi'a government there, Sunni leaders may feel coerced to formally recognize Israel's right to exist. As I write, the news has just broken that through the efforts of the Trump Administration, the United Arab Emirates has formally recognized Israel's right to exist, and entered into normal relations with Her!

Imagine how different the world will be under a 'Sunni dominated Middle East,' that has subdued Iran (the Chief State sponsor

of terror in the region), and recognized Israel's right to exist as a nation! The oil will flow unencumbered by warring factions in the region. The U.S., Russia, and China will have no justification for keeping troops there any longer, and prosperity will flow from this regional peace!

Indeed, this 'peace accord' which was FORETOLD in your Bible (DANIEL 9:27), will lull the people of Israel and probably most of the world asleep, thinking 'permanent peace' has finally come to one of the great trouble spots on earth, the Middle East. It will no doubt bring to pass this additional prophecy:

"MY HAND will be against the prophets who envision futility and who divine lies… because they have seduced MY people (Israel), **saying**, 'Peace! **When there is no peace**."

This 'peace accord' will be short-lived, because your Bible says that 'at the time of the end' the 'King of the North' (Little Horn – Turkey) will be attacked by the 'King of the South' (Egypt), and the 'King of the North' will come against him like a whirlwind, not only taking over Egypt, but many other Countries too, including Israel! (DANIEL 8:9-11; 11:41)

When the Arab Spring resulted in the election of a 'Muslim Brotherhood' candidate (Muhamad Morsi - June 2012), to the Presidency of Egypt, I was puzzled at the development. Why? Because the 'King of the North' (Prime Minister Erdogan) was supportive of the Muslim Brotherhood that brought Morsi to power. They were of kindred spirits! And I knew that the last 5 verses of Daniel chapter eleven revealed that these 2 kings had to be at odds with one another, for this prophecy about a war between them to be fulfilled.

Less than a year later, a coup occurred in Egypt that took the new Muslim Brotherhood President from power. When it happened, I remember telling people on radio that this had to occur for the Kings of the North and South to be at odds with one another in the 'latter days.' Erdogan, was one of the few world leaders to condemn the coup, and to this day he is very much at odds with the new 'King of the South,'Abdel Fattah El-Sisi!

THE 2300 DAYS PROPHECY

Since your Bible says that the '**Little Horn**' (DANIEL 8:12), and the '**King of the North**' (DANIEL 11:31), and '**a prince to come**' (DANIEL 9:26,27), all '**take away the daily sacrifices**,' they must be one and the same person, and it must be 'he' who takes the lead in both forging the peace covenant, and then breaking it halfway through the seven-year period (DANIEL 9:27)!

In order to '**take away the daily sacrifices**' in Israel, this sinister individual and his armies would have to take over and control Jerusalem. Your Bible forecasts that this 'fierce featured' king will do just that, in what is commonly called **the 2300 DAYS PROPHECY**:

"And it (**the Little Horn - Turkey**) grew up to the host of heaven (Angelic realm - I Kings 22:19); and **it cast down some of the host and some of the stars to the ground**, and trampled them. He even exalted himself as high as the Prince of the host; and by him the daily sacrifice was taken away and the place of HIS sanctuary was cast down. Because of transgression, an army was given over to 'the Horn,' to oppose the daily sacrifices; and he cast truth down to the ground. He did all this and prospered. Then I heard a holy one (Angel) speaking; and another holy one said to that certain one who was speaking, 'How long will the vision be, concerning the daily sacrifices and the transgression of desolation, **the giving of both the sanctuary and the host to be trampled underfoot**? And he said to me, 'For 2300 days; then the sanctuary shall be cleansed.' Then it happened, when I, Daniel, had seen the vision and was seeking the meaning, that suddenly there stood before me one having the appearance of a man. And I heard a man's voice between the banks of the Ulai (River), who called, and said, 'Gabriel, make this man understand the vision.' So he came near where I stood, and when he came I was afraid and fell on my face; but he said to me, 'Understand, son of man, that **the vision refers to the time of the End**.' (DANIEL 8:10-17 NKJV)

There's a lot to take notice of in order to understand this prophecy. First of all, nowhere in the text are we told to count 2300 days. Yet many interpretations of this text are based on counting 2300 days or years (invoking the day for a year principle - EZEKIEL 4:6), from the time the prophecy was given – to arrive at some dramatic event in the future. It is an Angel who asks another Angel, 'How long will the vision be?' that invokes the answer: 2300 days. And the Angel that gives the answer mentions 4 specific events that will occur within that 2300 days: **the Daily Sacrifices**, **the transgression of desolation**, **'the host' being trampled underfoot**, and **the Sanctuary being trampled underfoot** (DANIEL 8:13).

These are all 'end time' events according to your Bible, not past events associated with Daniel's day. **The Daily Sacrifices** are taken away amidst the end time 'Peace Accord' (DANIEL 9:27). Jesus said that 'when you see the **Abomination of Desolation** spoken of by Daniel the Prophet, standing in the Holy Place (which transgresses GOD'S Law against Idolatry), then there will be Great Tribulation – speaking of the unparalleled time of trouble leading up to His return. And as we'll see, the trampling of 'the host' and 'the Sanctuary' are also 'end time events.'

Throughout your Bible, **stars and hosts are symbols of the Angels in heaven**:

"When the morning stars sang together; and all the sons of God shouted for joy?" (JOB 38:7 NKJV)

"And suddenly there was with the Angel a multitude of the heavenly host praising GOD and saying: 'Glory to GOD in the highest, and on earth peace, good will toward men." (LUKE 2:13 NKJV)

But how could a human leader called the 'Little Horn' do battle with these 'host of heaven' and cast some to the ground – as the 2300 days prophecy says? Well, the answer is: 'he couldn't!' But remember that your Bible says that Satan is the power behind this leader's throne (DANIEL 8;23,24) (REVELATION 13:1,2). So the text is speaking metaphorically of the power behind the 'Little Horn' doing battle with the Angels (Host) of Heaven.

In the 10th chapter of the book of Daniel, we're given insight into the 'Spirit Realm,' in which it is revealed that **there are 'principalities and powers'** (As the Apostle Paul wrote: Ephesians 6:12) **behind the Human Thrones of this world**! An Angel tells Daniel:

"But the **Prince of Persia** withstood me (Gabriel) 21 days; and behold, Michael, one of the chief princes, came to help me, for I had been left alone there with the kings of Persia… And now I must return to fight with the prince of Persia; and when I have gone forth, indeed the **Prince of Greece** will come." (DANIEL 10:13,20)

According to the book of Deuteronomy, **the nations of the earth were apportioned among Angels**:

"THE MOST HIGH assigned nations their lands; HE determined where peoples should live. **HE assigned to each nation a heavenly being**, but Jacob's descendants (Israel) HE chose for HIMSELF." (DEUTERONOMY 32:8 GNT)

Most people don't see these spiritual powers behind the headlines they read – but they are there! And if all Humanities' eyes were opened to see the Angels and Demons behind Egypt, China, Germany, and the United States – they would instantly have a new paradigm of this world! If they could see the spiritual battles going on behind the thrones of this world's governments, they would better understand why there is so much conflict in the world! Elisha once prayed for his trembling servant to have his eyes opened by GOD to see these Angelic armies gathered all around them (II KINGS 6:17-20). Behind the scenes of Human Governments is where you'll find the true 'Game of Thrones!'

There's only one other place in your Bible that speaks of someone casting down stars (Angels) from heaven as we read in Daniel's 2300 DAY PROPHECY – and that's Satan the Devil – during a future war that breaks out in heaven:

"Another sign appeared in heaven: behold, a great fiery red dragon having 7 heads and 10 horns and 7 diadems on his heads

(Satan). **His tail drew a 1/3 of the stars** (Angels Rev.1:20) **of heaven and threw them to the earth… And war broke out in heaven**: Michael and his angels fought with the dragon; and the dragon and his angels fought, but they did not prevail, nor was a place found for them in heaven any longer." (REVELATION 12:3-8)

The Greek word 'Suro' (translated here in verse 4 as 'drew' is translated elsewhere in the New Testament 'drag' - as against one's will LUKE 12:58). The Greek word 'Ballo' (translated 'threw' here in verse 4), is an intense primary verb meant to convey casting or throwing violently (ACTS 16:23). Many have viewed this text as a past event in which Lucifer (who became the dragon) allured 1/3 of the Angels to his 'evil side.' But there's no alluring indicated here. Instead, there is the kind of violence associated with war! And verse 8 describes that war in detail, as a war between Angels and Demons.

Comparing this text with Daniel's 2300 DAY PROPHECY (8:10-17), it becomes clear that the '**trampling of the Heavenly Host underfoot**' is a yet future event. Indeed, Daniel is told by the Angel speaking with him, that '**the vision refers to the time of the End**.'

The 2300 DAY PROPHECY also says that **the Sanctuary will be trampled underfoot** at that time. Most people would associate 'the Sanctuary' with the Tabernacle or Temple, as that is how we find the word used most often in Scripture. But the first time you find the word sanctuary in your Bible, it has a much broader meaning:

"YOU will bring them (Israel) in and plant them in the mountain of your inheritance (**Zion, Jerusalem** – Isaiah 40:9), in the place O LORD, which you have made for YOUR own dwelling, **The Sanctuary**, O LORD, which YOUR HANDS have established." (EXODUS 15:17 NKJV)

GOD'S SANCTUARY originally referred to Jerusalem at large - not just the Temple grounds. So when Daniel is told that **the place of HIS sanctuary was cast down** by the 'Little Horn' (DANIEL 8:11) – he was meant to understand that the Angel was speaking of Zion – the Sanctuary or dwelling place of THE LORD.

And that is exactly what the Apostle John was told would happen to the Holy Sanctuary of GOD, under the reign of **the Beast**:

"Then I was given a reed like a measuring rod. And the Angel stood, saying, 'Rise and measure the temple of GOD (The Church – I CORINTHIANS 3:16,17), and those who worship there. But leave out the court which is outside the temple, and do not measure it, for it has been given to **the Gentiles** (unbelievers). **And they will tread the Holy City underfoot for 42 months**." (REVELATION 11:1,2 NKJV)

The 2300 DAYS PROPHECY culminates in the 'cleansing of the sanctuary' (DANIEL 8:14), which is the cleansing of Jerusalem by Christ at His return:

"In that Day, the Branch (Christ) of THE LORD shall be beautiful and glorious; and the fruit of the earth shall be excellent and appealing for those of Israel who have escaped. And it shall come to pass that he who is left in Zion and remains in Jerusalem will be called holy – everyone who is recorded among the living in

Jerusalem. When THE LORD has **washed away the filth of the daughters of Zion**, and **purged the bloodshed of Jerusalem from her midst**, by the spirit of judgment and by the spirit of burning." (ISAIAH 4:2-4 NKJV)

John's vision says that the Holy City (GOD'S Sanctuary) will be tread underfoot for 42 months, which equals 1260 days (42x30days in the Hebrew Lunar month = 1260). **Daniel is told by Michael the Archangel that "From the time that the Daily Sacrifice is taken away, and the Abomination of Desolation is set up, there shall be 1290 days." (DANIEL** 12:11) This is part of the last 2300 days leading up to Christ's return.

Daniel's visions speaks **not only about the Sanctuary** (Jerusalem) **being tread underfoot – but also the host of heaven** (Angels) **being cast down to the earth and trampled underfoot** - a combination of events which takes 2300 literal days (DANIEL 8:13,14).

Subtracting the 1260 days for the trampling of the Sanctuary (Jerusalem) underfoot, from the 2300 DAY PROPHECY leaves 1040 days for the trampling of the heavenly host by Satan the Devil, which happens first.

We saw in the book of Daniel (chapter 10) how one battle between one Angel of GOD and the Prince of Persia lasted 21 days. **This final climactic battle in heaven between Michael and his Angels and Satan and his demons** (Revelation 12:7-13), **during which time Satan casts 1/3 of the heavenly host of Angels to the ground (trampling), lasts 1040 days!** It culminates in Satan and his angels finally being defeated – and forever banned from the heavens thereafter:

"Now when the dragon saw that he had been cast to the earth, he persecuted the woman (Israel) who gave birth to the male child (Jesus)." (REVELATION 12:13 NKJV)

This is when the Devil empowers the 'Little Horn' to **enter the Glorious Land of Israel**, **take away the 'daily sacrifice,' and tread the Holy City underfoot for 42 months** or 1260 days.

Will mankind notice the Heavenly battle? It may manifest itself in what looks like an on-going meteor shower, as the stars of heaven (Angels – JOB 38:7) are cast down to the ground by Satan.

Woe to those who walk the earth when the Devil himself is cast down, '**having great wrath**, **because he knows that he has a short time.**' (REVELATION 12:12)

CHAPTER 10
'THE BEAST'

Your Bible speaks of several great mysteries, which only those who have GOD'S HOLY SPIRIT can unravel and understand (I Corinthians 2:11)! The Apostle Paul speaks about one of those mysteries in a letter to the Church at Thessalonica:

> "For THE MYSTERY of LAWLESSNESS is already at work; only he who now restrains will do so until he is taken out of the way. Then THE LAWLESS ONE will be revealed, whom THE LORD will consume with the breath of His mouth and destroy with the brightness of His coming. **The coming of THE LAWLESS ONE is according to the working of Satan, with all power, signs, and lying wonders, and with all unrighteous deception among those who perish, because they did not receive the love of the truth, that they might be saved**. And for this reason, GOD will send them strong delusion, that they should believe the lie, that they all may be condemned who did not believe the truth, but had pleasure in unrighteousness. (II THESSALONIANS 2:8-12)

Paul is describing the same sinister leader we've been talking about in previous chapters, the '**Little Horn**,' and '**the Beast**,' whose power is also said to come from Satan (DANIEL 8:24) (REV.13:2). He will be destroyed by Christ at His 2nd Coming (DANIEL 8:25) (REV.19:20).

The world has seen many 'Regional Empires' come and go, including that of Genghis Khan, who carved out the most extensive geographical empire in history, conquering most of Asia, Eastern Europe, and the Middle East.

But the one Paul calls, '**The Lawless One**,' **will forge the first Global Empire in history**:

"Then I (the Apostle John) stood on the sand of the Sea. And I saw **a Beast rising up** out of the Sea, **having 7 heads & 10 Horns**, and on his horns a blasphemous name. Now **the Beast** which I saw was like a leopard, his feet were like the feet of a bear, and his mouth like the mouth of a lion. **The Dragon** (Satan) **gave him his power**, **his throne and great authority**. And I saw one of the (7) heads as if it had been mortally wounded, and his deadly wound was healed. And **all the world marveled and followed the Beast. So they worshiped the dragon**, **who gave authority to the Beast**; and they worshiped the Beast, saying, 'Who is like the Beast? Who is able to make war with him? **And he was given a mouth speaking great things and blasphemies** and **he was given authority to continue for 42 months**. Then he opened his mouth in blasphemy against GOD, to blaspheme HIS NAME, HIS TABERNACLE, and those who dwell in heaven. **It was granted to him to make war with the Saints and to overcome them, and authority was given him over every tribe, tongue, and nation**." (REVELATION 13:1-7 NKJV)

No kingdom in history has ever ruled over every tribe, tongue, and nation on this earth – but this one will – thankfully for only 3 ½ years (42 months)! The tentacles of Islam (almost 2 billion) stretch around the world to every tribe, tongue, and nation. And all it would take to unite them as one massive army wreaking havoc in every city on earth – is a charismatic leader empowered by Satan to work 'signs and lying wonders'- which 'The Beast' and this 'Lawless One' are prophesied to do!

Notice that 'The Beast' speaks blasphemies against GOD ALMIGHTY – just as we read about 'The Lawless One' who declares himself as God (II Thessalonians 2:4) and the 'Little Horn' who blasphemes THE MOST HIGH (Daniel 7:25).

This 7-headed Beast incorporates all 4 of the Beasts of Daniel's vision (DANIEL 7:1-7): The Lion (Babylonian Empire); The Bear (Medo-Persian Empire), The Leopard (Greece); and the 4th Beast described as 'dreadful & terrible' which had 10 Horns.

But that only accounts for four of the seven heads of this 7-headed Beast. What about the three other heads? We get a broader explanation in the 17th chapter of the book of Revelation:

"Here is the mind which has wisdom: The 7 heads (of the 7-headed Beast in chapter 13) are 7 mountains (symbolic of empires – Isaiah 13:4) on which the woman (Harlot) sits. There are also 7 Kings (tying kingdoms to mountains). **Five have fallen** (The Egyptian, Assyrian, Babylonian, Medo-Persian and Greek Empires as of John's writing), **One is** (John was living under the Roman Empire) and **the other has not yet come** (The Islamic Empire). And when he comes, he must continue a short time. **The Beast that was**, **and is not, is himself also the**

8th, **and is of the 7**, **and is going to perdition** (destruction). **The 10 Horns which you saw are 10 Kings who have received no kingdom as yet,** but they receive authority for one hour as Kings with 'the Beast.' These are of one mind, and they will give their power and authority to 'The Beast.' These will make war with 'The Lamb' (Jesus), and 'The Lamb' will overcome them…" (REVELATION 17:9-14)

Daniel, the Prophet, was given visions of empires beginning with the one he was living under Nebuchadnezzar's Babylon. The Apostle John was also given visions of empires, including the one he was living under (Rome). But the vision given to John included five previous kingdoms and one that had not yet come.

THE 8TH KINGDOM

The burning question that comes from this text is **which of these 7 Kingdoms will rise again as the 8th and final Kingdom?**

The answer: The only one of the seven previous kingdoms which **reach into every tribe**, **tongue**, **and nation** today (REV.13:7); the only one of the seven previous kingdoms **causing terror** all over the world today (EZEKIEL 32); the only one of the seven previous kingdoms **persecuting 'the Saints'** all over the world today (REV.13:7); the only one of the seven previous kingdoms involved in **Human Trafficking** all over the world today (REV.18:13); the only one of the seven previous kingdoms **beheading** 'the Saints' all over the world today (REV.20:4) – **RADICAL ISLAM!**

The color of the Beast is 'Scarlet' (REV.17:3), and nations are proudly represented by colors in their flags. It's significant that the nation of Turkey has a scarlet red flag with a white crescent moon and white star. We have seen already that the King of the North was headquartered in Antioch, Turkey, Satan's throne is in Turkey, and Gog was the chief prince of 2 regions of Turkey, called Meshech and Tubal.

These are the Biblical signs identifying the end-time Beast that rules over the whole world – and most Christians are completely unaware of them! What the Apostle John wrote about the 'Anti-Christ' also points to the religion of Islam:

"He is Anti-Christ who denies THE FATHER and the Son." (I JOHN 2:22 NKJV)

Over a dozen times in the Quran, the reader is warned against associating anything or anyone with its god. The Quran says: "He (**Allah**) whose is the kingdom of the heavens and the earth and who **did NOT take to himself a son** and who has no associate in the kingdom." (Surah 25:2)

The FATHER-Son relationship is of paramount importance in Christianity! The Bible says we are made in GOD'S IMAGE and LIKENESS (GENESIS 1:27) and that through the resurrection from the dead, we will become HIS eternal children (I CORINTHIANS 15:50-53) (I JOHN 3:1,2).

Such concepts are anathema to Muslims, who think that associating 'familial terms' with Deity diminishes God to Human levels. Yet nominal Christians and Muslims believe they worship the same God!

There are many more prophecies in your Bible that make it clear that **it is the 7th head of the 7 Headed Beast** (The Islamic Empire) **that will rise again and become 'the 8th'– not any of the previous six**.

WHAT NATIONS WILL CHRIST FIGHT AT HIS RETURN?

If you look at the Biblical texts about which peoples Christ fights at His return, they're all Muslim nations today:

"The utterance of him (Balaam) who hears the words of GOD, and has the knowledge of THE MOST HIGH, who sees the vision of THE ALMIGHTY, who falls down, with eyes wide open: 'I see Him (the promised Messiah), but not now; I behold Him, but not near; A Star (Jesus – MT.2:2) shall come out of Jacob; A Scepter (HEB.1:8) shall rise out of Israel and batter the brow of Moab (**Modern day Jordan**), and destroy all the sons of tumult. And Edom (**Southern Jordan**) shall be a possession; Seir (**SouthJordan**) also, his enemies, shall be a possession, while Israel does valiantly." (NUMBERS 24:16-18)

"A prophecy against Egypt (The King of the South): See, **THE LORD rides on a swift cloud** (MT.24:30) **and is coming to Egypt**. The idols of Egypt tremble before Him, and the hearts of the Egyptians melt with fear." (ISAIAH 19:1,2 NIV)

"For through the Voice of THE LORD (Christ – DT.18:18) Assyria (**Modern Day Syria**, **Turkey**, **Iran & Iraq**) will be beaten down, as He strikes with the rod (REV.19:15)." (ISAIAH 30:31)

There are no references to Christ fighting Rome, or Germany, or Russia at His return, but Scripture does tell us He will fight Egypt, Syria, Jordan, Turkey, Iran, and Iraq at His return!

THE 'MARK' of THE BEAST

Much speculation has been made about '**the mark of the Beast**,' and what clues it may give in determining the identity of this enigmatic figure and his empire:

"He causes all, both small and great, rich and poor, free and slave, to receive a **mark on their right hand or on their foreheads**, and that no one can buy or sell except one has the mark or the name of the Beast, or the number of his name. Here is wisdom, let him who has understanding calculate the number of the Beast, **for it is the number of a man**; **His number is 666**." (REVELATION 13:16-18 NKJV)

The mark of the Beast is the number of 'Man' (GK. Anthropos), who was created on the 6th Day of Creation, out of carbon (the 6th element on the Periodic Table). The placement of the mark on the right hand or forehead is symbolic of the 2 centers of work, the brain (white collar) and the hand (blue-collar).

GOD THE FATHER set aside the 7th day of the week (GENESIS 2:2,3) for Man to cease from work and worship his CREATOR. The Catholic Church changed the day Man should cease from work to the 1st day of the week, Sunday. Muhammad chose to declare that Man's rest day should be the 6th day of the week.

This is no small matter! The 'Little Horn' whom Scripture equates with 'the Beast,' as we have seen, "…shall speak pompous words against THE MOST HIGH, shall persecute the Saints of THE MOST HIGH, and shall intend to change **times** and **law**." (DANIEL 7:25)

As Islam has expanded around the world, it has sought to change times (the cycle of the workweek to Saturday through Thursday, resting on Friday the 6th day, as well as the annual observance of Ramadan) and law (Establishing and invoking Sharia Law and Courts within their communities).

When Islam gains authority '**over every tribe**, **tongue**, **and nation**' (REV.13:7), through the conquering Beast, their work cycle will likely become the world's norm – and anyone who doesn't embrace it won't be able to 'buy or sell!' (REVELATION 13:17)

The Quran discusses the importance to be placed on observing Friday as a holy day:

> "O you who believe! When you are called to congregational (Arabic: Al-Jumah, Friday) prayer, hasten to the remembrance of God **and leave off trade**. That is better for you, if you but knew." (Surah 62:9)

The only effect of 'the mark of the Beast' given in the discussion of it in the 13th chapter of the book of Revelation – is not being able to 'buy or sell' without it. Islam's commandeering of the 6th day of the week (the number of Man, GEN.1:27,31) as the official 'day of ceasing commerce' outlaws white-collar work (Forehead) and blue-collar work (hand) on that day. Under the final Caliphate of 'the Beast,' the embracing of Islam's work cycle will determine whether one can do business or not!

The rise of Islam to its height of geographical dominance under the Umayyad Caliphate, around 666 A.D. – associates this number with the Muslim Religion. I say 'around 666 A.D.' – because historical records are not certain, in pinpointing the exact Zenith of the Umayyad Caliphate.

Is it only coincidental that the world's 2nd largest Religion arose in this particular century? Why not the 2nd or 10th century? No other major Religion or Movement in the world began in the 600'S A.D.

The symbol of Islam is the 'Crescent Moon' (New Moon) found on many of its flags and minarets. The GOD of the Bible says that this 'New Moon' will be used to punish Israel:

"They (Israel) have dealt treacherously with THE LORD, for they have begotten pagan (worldly) children. **Now a 'New Moon' shall devour them and their heritage.**" (HOSEA 5:7 NKJV)

The 'Little Horn' (Daniel 8:9-14), who is also 'The King of the North' (Daniel 11:40-42), and Gog (Ezekiel 38:8), and 'The Beast' (Revelation 11:1-7) – bearer of the 'New Crescent Moon,' is prophesied to enter the Land of Israel, and tread it underfoot for 42 months (Rev.11:2)!

CHAPTER 11
'THE GREAT HARLOT'

When a woman sits upon a beast (Horse, Ox, Camel) – it's to take authority over that animal and make it move in the direction she wants it to go. The animal has a mind of its own, however, so the woman must put reigns upon its mouth and head, to steer it, and let it know who's in charge.

In your Bible, a woman is symbolic of 'Religion.' The Apostle Paul refers to the Church (which represents the Christian Religion) as '**the wife**' of Christ (Ephesians 5:22-32). The Apostle John also refers to the Congregation of Israel as '**the woman who gave birth to the male Child**.' (Revelation 12:5)

So when John also writes of '**a woman sitting on a scarlet beast**,' the reader should understand that he is speaking of **a Religious Institution steering and controlling a secular Beast**:

"I (an Angel) will show you (John) the judgment of '**The Great Harlot' who sits on many waters** (**Nations** – Isaiah 17:12,13), with whom the kings of the earth committed fornication, and the inhabitants of the earth were made drunk with the wine of her fornication. So he carried me away in THE SPIRIT into the wilderness. And I saw **a woman sitting on a scarlet Beast** which was full of names of blasphemy, having 7 Heads and 10 Horns. The woman was **arrayed in purple and scarlet, and adorned with gold and precious stones and pearls, having in her hand a golden cup** full of abominations and the filthiness of her fornication, and on her forehead a name was written: **MYSTERY, BABYLON THE GREAT, THE MOTHER OF HARLOTS AND OF THE ABOMINATIONS OF THE EARTH**. I saw the woman, drunk with the blood of the Saints and with the blood of the martyrs of Jesus…" (REV.17:1-6 NKJV)

Like 'the Beast' She rides (REV.13:7), this 'False Religious Institution' martyrs the Saints of the Christian Religion. This Woman also has something the nations of the earth want, and they are willing to enter into fornication (mutual pleasure), to get it. And She is well adorned, the picture of wealth. Yet She is blasphemous in the mind of the GOD of the Bible, misappropriating HIS NAMES, and luring the nations away from their TRUE CREATOR!

THE IDENTITY of 'THE GREAT HARLOT'

Another important detail about 'The Great Harlot' is given in the last verse of the 17th chapter of the book of Revelation:

> "**And the Woman whom you saw is that great city which reigns over the kings of the earth**." (REVELATION 17:18 NKJV)

Remember that 'The Great Harlot' sits upon the '7 Headed Beast with 10 Horns.' That Beast, as we discovered in the last chapter, represents seven successive kingdoms that have all come and gone: The Egyptian, Assyrian, Babylonian, Medo-Persian, Greek,

Roman, and Muslim Empires. So which city in Human History can be said to have 'sat upon' or steered in some way, these seven kingdoms? The answer is found in the first book of your Bible!

The book of Genesis tells us that after the flood, the earth's population was all grouped together in Mesopotamia, ignoring GOD'S command to: '…Be fruitful and multiply; Fill the earth and subdue it.' (GENESIS 1:28).

Instead, the people said,

'Come let us build ourselves a CITY, and a tower whose top is in the heavens; let us make a name for ourselves, lest we be scattered abroad over the face of the whole earth." (GENESIS 11:4 NKJV)

The name of that city they built was called BABEL. It was here that GOD divided mankind, by giving each ethnic group a distinct language and leading them with Angels to their respective borders.

Israel was warned by GOD:

"Take heed, lest you lift your eyes to heaven, and when you see **the sun, the moon and the stars**, all the host of heaven, you feel driven to worship them and serve them, **which THE LORD your GOD has given to all the peoples under the whole heaven as a heritage**." (DEUTERONOMY 4:19 NKJV)

History reveals that all these different peoples who became nations through the Divine Act of language implanting, took with them as they dispersed around the world, **the Astrological Worship System** they learned at Babel.

Through this migration, the City of Babel mothered, or gave birth to 'Harlot Cities' all over the world! These cities became the 'Religious Centers' of each Kingdom, where the various ethnic groups continued to worship the sun, moon, and stars – including the seven kingdoms of the 7 Headed Beast. **Thus her title was given to her** (Babel) **in the book of Revelation: MYSTERY BABYLON THE GREAT, THE MOTHER OF HARLOTS AND OF THE ABOMINATIONS OF THE EARTH.**

Sumerian History records the practice of kings gaining their legitimacy by having sex with the temple prostitute in these cities on New Year's Eve – setting up **a pattern of kings of the earth committing fornication with the temple harlot** (Revelation 17:2), and demonstrating the subservience of the 'Secular Branch of Government' to the Religious Hierarchy and its gods.

THE 1st HARLOT DAUGHTER OF BABEL

In Egypt, the ancient city of Memphis (called 'Noph' in your Bible) became **the first daughter harlot of Babel** to ride or steer the 1st Head of the 7-Headed Beast:

> "Thus says THE LORD GOD: 'I will also destroy the idols, and cause the images to cease from Noph (Memphis, Egypt)." (EZEKIEL 30:13 NKJV)

> "O **you daughter** (of Babel?) dwelling in Egypt, prepare yourself to go into captivity! For Noph shall be waste and desolate, without inhabitant." (JEREMIAH 46:19 NKJV)

Noph, or Memphis, was the Religious Center of Egypt for centuries. Even though the Pharaohs of Egypt were considered gods themselves – they were subservient to and did obeisance to Ra, the Sun god, and Hathor, who was considered their mother. This religious city steered the moral and spiritual direction of Egypt and her kings.

The 2nd HARLOT DAUGHTER OF BABEL

In the Kingdom of Assyria, **the city of Nineveh was the daughter harlot of Babel** that rode or steered the 2nd Head of the 7-Headed Beast:

> "Because of **the multitude of harlotries of the seductive harlot** (Nineveh), the Mistress of Sorceries, who sells nations through her harlotries and families through her sorceries. (NAHUM 3:4 NKJV)

Many are not aware that someone hundred years after the city of Nineveh repented at Jonah's preaching, the next generation of Ninevites had become so corrupt that GOD sent a second prophet, Nahum, to warn them once again of impending Divine Judgment. So strong was their attachment to the harlotries of their temple city, that this time they ignored the warning, and GOD used one of their enemies to wipe them off the face of the map! Read this 3 chapter book and see the detailed description of this Harlot City of Nineveh.

THE 3rd HARLOT DAUGHTER OF BABEL

The Kingdoms of Babylon and Persia (represented by the 3rd & 4th Heads of the 7-Headed Beast) **were ridden by the updated version of the Mother City of Babel – Babylon**! Her harlotry is well documented in the pages of the book of Daniel:

"Nebuchadnezzar the king made an image of gold, whose height was 60 cubits and its width 6 cubits. He set it up in the plain of Dura, **in the province of Babylon**… Then a herald cried aloud: 'To you it is commanded, O peoples, nations, and languages, that at the time you hear the sound of the horn, flute, harp, lyre, and psaltery, in symphony with all kinds of music, **you shall fall down and worship the gold image** that King Nebuchadnezzar has set up; and whoever does not fall down and worship shall be cast immediately into the midst of a burning fiery furnace." (DANIEL 3:1,4,5 NKJV)

Such blatant idolatry was one of the reasons The Babylonian Empire was so short-lived. The old saying, 'The handwriting is on the wall,' originated in your Bible, when an Angel wrote a fatalistic message to the last king of the Babylonian Empire, saying:

"GOD has numbered your kingdom, and finished it; you have been weighed in the (moral) balances, and found wanting; your kingdom has been divided, and given to the Medes and Persians." (DANIEL 5:26-28 NKJV)

THE 4TH HARLOT DAUGHTER OF BABEL

The Kingdom of Greece (represented by the 5th Head of the 7-Headed Beast) **was steered by that great Harlot City of Athens**. The book of ACTS records the Apostle Paul's visit to this city:

"Now while Paul waited for them at **Athens**, his spirit was provoked within him when he saw that **the city was given over to idols**…" (ACTS 17:16 NKJV)

Greek Mythology is known the world over! Study of the History of this nation shows how strongly influenced she was by Athens and her gods, representing the sun, moon, and stars – just as her mother, Babel.

THE 5TH HARLOT DAUGHTER OF BABEL

The Roman Empire (represented by the 6th Head of the 7-Headed Beast) **was ridden by the Harlot City of Rome**. The Roman Pantheon of gods also revolved around the sun, moon, and stars like its predecessors. It is believed by some theologians that the Apostle Peter used the metonym 'Babylon' in describing Rome as a Harlot City:

> "She (the Church) who is in Babylon (Rome), elect together with you, greets you; and so does Mark my son." (I PETER 5:13 NKJV)

Remember the Apostle John was told in reference to the 7-Headed Beast, that 5 of the 7 heads (kingdoms) of the 7-Headed Beast 'had fallen' (Rev.17:10), 'one is' – John was living under the Roman Empire – so it was likely well known among the 'Original Christians' that Rome was the 'new Babylon,' or Harlot City – riding the 6th Head of the 7-Headed Beast.

THE 6TH DAUGHTER HARLOT OF BABEL

From the time of Constantine's Edict of Milan in 313 A.D., making Christianity the Official Religion of the Empire, **the Papacy of Vatican City steered** this 6th Head of the 7-Headed Beast – crowning kings 'Head' of the Holy Roman Empire for centuries, clear up to 'the ride' of Napoleon Bonaparte.

The union of Church and State was made famous or infamous during the reign of THE HOLY ROMAN EMPIRE!

THE 7TH DAUGHTER HARLOT OF BABEL

The Islamic Empire, which swallowed up 2/3 of the Holy Roman Empire, **was ridden and steered by the City of Mecca** from the 7th Century till the 20th Century. Prayers were directed towards Her five times a day by Muslims all over the world.

When Muhammad came on the world scene, there were 360 gods worshiped at the Kaaba Stone in Mecca – with the moon god, being the Chief Deity. The name of the Moon god was 'Sin' and was used by the Arabs in naming the region of Sinai. Muhammad replaced the pantheon of gods with one god he called 'Allah' – but retained the pagan symbol of the crescent moon, which is displayed prominently on Islamic flags, Mosques, and Minarets all over the world.

Throughout history, the power that gave the secular thrones of this world their authority were the gods set up and worshiped in these 'Harlot Cities.' Thus these Religious Cities, who were daughters of the city of Babel, in that they all worshiped the 'heavenly host of Astral bodies' their forefathers did in that post-flood city, 'sat upon' or steered the 7 Middle Eastern Empires called the 7-Headed Beast in the book of Revelation!

The final Harlot City

As we learned in the last chapter, one of those 7 Heads or kingdoms will rise again and become the 8th and final empire. The Biblical evidence overwhelmingly points to the resurrection of the Islamic Empire.

Two whole chapters of the Old Testament (Jeremiah 50 & 51) and two whole chapters of the New Testament (Revelation 17 &

18) are devoted to the significant influence and ultimate demise of the Harlot City that rides that 8th and final Head of 'the Beast.'

What does your Bible reveal about the identity of the final Harlot city? Consider these verses:

"O **you** (Mecca?) **who dwell by many waters** (Red Sea, Arabian Sea, the Persian Gulf), abundant in treasures (Crude Oil?), your end has come, the measure of your covetousness." (JEREMIAH 51:13 NKJV)

"**The** (Red?) **Sea will rise over Babylon** (Mecca is 43 miles inland); its roaring waves will cover her." (JER.51:42)

"**A prophecy against the Desert by the Sea** (Saudi Arabia): Like whirlwinds sweeping through the southland (Arabia is in the South), an invader comes from the desert, from a land of terror. A dire vision has been shown to me: The traitor betrays, the looter takes loot. Elam (Southern Iran) attack! Media (Northern Iran), lay siege! I (THE LORD) will bring to an end all the groaning She (Babylon-Mecca) caused… '**Babylon has fallen, has fallen**!' All the images of its gods lie shattered on the ground. (ISAIAH 21:1,2,9 NIV)

"**And Babylon** (Mecca), the glory of kingdoms, the beauty of the Chaldeans' pride, **will be as when GOD overthrew Sodom and Gomorrah**. It will never be inhabited, nor will it be settled from generation to generation; **Nor will the Arabian pitch tents there**…" (ISAIAH 13:19,20 NKJV)

Amid the discussion of Babylon and its fate in chapters 50 & 51 of the book of Jeremiah, she is referred to as 'the daughter of

Babel' twice (50:42, 51:33). Remember, we're told in the book of Revelation that BABYLON THE GREAT (Babel) is the mother of HARLOTS. We've seen from the pages of your Bible that **Babel sired many daughter cities like herself**, devoted to the worship of the Astral bodies in the heavens: Noph (Memphis), Nineveh, Babylon, Athens, Rome, Vatican City, and Mecca (that worships the Moon god).

The final Harlot City that rides the 8th Head of the Beast is identified with the following characteristics: dwelling by many waters; abundant in treasures; covered by the waves of the Sea at Her demise; a land in the Desert by the Sea; Arabians will no longer pitch their tents there.

Combined together, these texts point to Mecca as that final Harlot City! She dwells '**by many waters**,' on the Arabian peninsula, which is surrounded by waters on three sides.

Saudi Arabia is **abundant in treasures**, being 2nd only to the United States in the generation of oil. She also produces natural gas, gold, copper, and iron ore. Mecca recently built the largest building in terms of volume ever built (Mecca Clock Tower), at the cost of 15 billion dollars!

Another overlooked clue is this statement the Angel makes to John about the final Harlot City:

> "**For all the nations have drunk of the wine of the wrath of her fornication**, the kings of the earth have committed fornication with her, and the merchants of the earth have become rich through the abundance of her luxury." (REVELATION 18:3 NKJV)

If you ever get to see 'crude oil' in a wine glass – you will think it is a burgundy! ALMIGHTY GOD made sure that oil became the engine of the world's economy so that Mecca and Her Islamic OPEC partners would become rich and powerful in the 'Latter Days'!

Most of the nations on earth buy oil from Saudi Arabia, and in return, the Saudi's not only growing rich, but they get to build Mosques in the Countries they sell to, expanding the reach and impact of Islam around the world! There's an old Islamic proverb that reads:

"The Mosques are our **barracks**; the minarets our **bayonets**; the domes our **helmets** and the faithful our soldiers."

National oil purchases from the Saudi's insures the armies of 'Radical Islam' will be in place to bring **every tribe**, **tongue and nation under the authority of** 'the Beast!' (REVELATION 13:7)

The good news (Gospel) is that She (the Harlot) who rides (the Beast) will have a short reign, and be overthrown:

"I (THE LORD) will punish Bel (Arabian god) in Babylon, and I will bring out of his mouth what he has swallowed; and the nations shall not stream to him anymore. (**Mecca is the single most visited spot on earth**). Yes the wall of Babylon shall fall." (JEREMIAH 51:44 NKJV)

ZECHARIAH'S 7th VISION

Zechariah's 7th Vision is about this daughter of 'Babel' (The Mother of Harlots) being returned to She who birthed her:

"Then the messenger speaking with me came forward and said, 'Look up and see what's approaching.' I said, 'What's this?' He said, '**This is the basket that is going out**. This is how it appears **throughout the entire land** (Hebrew 'Erets' - **earth**).' Then a lead cover was lifted, showing **a woman sitting in the middle of the basket**. He said, '**This is wickedness**.' He shoved her back into the basket, and he put the lead stone over its opening. I looked up again and saw 2 women going out. There was a wind in their wings; their wings were like the wings of a stork. **They carried the basket between the earth and the sky**. I said to the messenger speaking with me, 'Where are they taking the basket?' He said to me, '**To build a house for it in the Land of Shinar**. It will be firmly placed there on its base.'" (Zechariah 5:5-11 CEB)

Remember that in your Bible – a woman is symbolic of 'religion.' **The woman sitting in the basket is referred to by the messenger as**: 'Wickedness.'

The Great Harlot who rides the Beast and 'sits upon many waters' (nations), **is the epitome of wickedness**, described in John's vision as being:

"…Arrayed in purple and scarlet, and adorned with gold and precious stones and pearls, having in her hand a golden cup **full of abominations and the filthiness of her fornication**.' (REVELATION 17:4 NKJV)

At the center of the Grand Mosque in Mecca is the Kaaba Stone, which has a 300 kg gold door, and a rain spout made of gold. The tapestry, which adorns the Kaaba Stone like a woman's dress (called the Kiswah) is made of 670 kg of silk. The embroidery upon it contains 15 kg. of gold threads. The current cost to manufacture it is almost five million dollars. Every year it is removed and cut into small pieces and given to visiting foreign Muslim dignitaries and organizations. (Wikipedia)

Zechariah is given a vision of this woman, symbolizing 'false religion,' being carried back to her place of origin – Babel (The Mother of Harlot Cities) – located in the Land of Shinar (GENESIS 11:1-9) – for the whole world to see (ZECHARIAH 5:6)! Maybe it will be there during the entire 1000 year reign of Christ, to remind all nations of how mankind had become seduced by the Great Harlot City of false religion.

And she is carried there by 2 other women, possibly symbolizing the True Religions of Judaism (Old Testament), and Christianity (New Testament).

GODSPEED that day!

CHAPTER 12
ZECHARIAH'S 3RD VISION

Humanity has been living through the period pictured by the Prophet Zechariah's first vision, **when all the earth is resting quietly – because of the COVID-19 shutdown of nations around the world**.

Zechariah's 2nd Vision is about the '**Little Horn**' (also known as Gog, the King of the North, and the Beast, as we've seen in the last few chapters) **plucking up and subduing 3 horns** (Syria, Iran, Iraq) and consolidating into '**4 Horns**.'

In Zechariah's 3rd Vision, these 4 Horns now representing the territory of the original King of the North (see the map of Seleucid Kingdom, chapter 7), invade the Land of Israel:

"Then I raised my eyes and looked, and behold, **a man with a measuring line in his hand**. So I said, 'Where are you going?' And he said to me, 'To measure Jerusalem, to see what is its width and what is its length…Up, up! **Flee from the Land of the North**,' says THE LORD; for I have spread you (Israel) abroad like the 4 winds of heaven,' says THE LORD. Up, Zion (Jerusalem)! Escape, you who dwell with **the daughter of Babylon**.' For thus says THE LORD of HOSTS: 'HE (the

FATHER) sent Me (Christ) after glory, to the nations which plunder you (**Jerusalem**); For he who touches you touches **the apple of HIS EYE**." (ZECHARIAH 2:1,2, 6-8 NKJV)

Remember from the last chapter, that the Beast (Kingdom of the North) is ridden by one of the daughter cities of Babel: Mecca – in the 'Last Days.' The inhabitants of Jerusalem who survive this Gentile invasion will be dwelling with the daughter of Babylon, who rides the Beast right into their city!

WHY GOD ALLOWS MODERN-DAY ISRAEL TO BE INVADED

Why will ALMIGHTY GOD allow Israel to be invaded once more - since She is called **the apple of GOD'S EYE**? (Deuteronomy 32:1)

The answer lies in the meaning of 'measuring' in the Old Testament. The Prophet Isaiah was inspired to write:

"Also I will make justice **the measuring line**, and righteousness **the plummet** (weight attached to line measuring perpendicularity).

GOD uses 'justice' and 'righteousness' as standards when measuring the moral state of peoples. And when the iniquity of a State or Nation reaches a certain boiling point, our CREATOR punishes those people either through natural disasters (JOB 37:9-13), famine (EZEKIEL14:13) pestilence (II CHRONICLES 7:13), or through the military actions of another nation (ISAIAH 10:5,6).

In the first chapter, we read of the cyclical punishment of Ancient Israel that resulted in her being plucked up from her land because of Her sins!

The books of the Kings and Chronicles are records of the many times and numerous ways that ALMIGHTY GOD punished Israel, and then delivered Her out of trouble when She repented.

Your Bible records the remorseful prayers of National Repentance by Ezra, Nehemiah, and the Prophet Daniel.

A U.S. PRAYER OF NATIONAL REPENTANCE

During the Civil War – President Abraham Lincoln prayed a prayer of National Repentance on behalf of the United States:

"A Proclamation.

Whereas, the Senate of the United States, devoutly recognizing the Supreme Authority and just Government of Almighty God, in all the affairs of men and of nations, has, by a resolution, requested the President to designate and set apart a day for National prayer and humiliation.

And whereas it is the duty of nations as well as of men, to own their dependence upon the overruling power of God, to confess their sins and transgressions, in humble sorrow, yet with assured hope that genuine repentance will lead to mercy and pardon; and to recognize the sublime truth, announced in the Holy Scriptures and proven by all history, that those nations only are blessed whose God is the Lord.

And, insomuch as we know that, by His divine law, nations like individuals are subjected to punishments and chastisements in this world, may we not justly fear that the awful calamity of civil war, which now desolates the land, may be but a punishment, inflicted upon us, for our presumptuous sins, to the needful end of our national reformation as a whole People? We have been the recipients of the choicest bounties of Heaven. We have been preserved, these many years, in peace and prosperity. We have grown in numbers, wealth and power, as no other nation has ever grown. But we have forgotten God. We have forgotten the gracious hand which preserved us in peace, and multiplied and enriched and strengthened us; and we have vainly imagined, in the deceitfulness of our hearts, that all these blessings were produced by some superior wisdom and virtue of our own. Intoxicated with unbroken success, we have become too self-sufficient to feel the necessity of redeeming and preserving grace, too proud to pray to the God that made us!

It behooves us then to humble ourselves before the offended Power, to confess our national sins, and to pray for clemency and forgiveness.

Now, therefore, in compliance with the request and fully concurring in the views of the Senate, I do, by this my proclamation, designate and set apart Thursday, the 30th. day of April, 1863, as a day of national humiliation, fasting and prayer. And I do hereby request all the People to abstain, on that day, from their ordinary secular pursuits, and to unite, at their several places of public worship and their respective homes, in keeping the day holy to the Lord, and devoted to the humble discharge of the religious duties proper to that solemn occasion.

All this being done, in sincerity and truth, let us then rest humbly in the hope authorized by the Divine teachings, that the united cry of the Nation will be heard on high, and answered with blessings, no less than the pardon of our national sins, and the restoration of our now divided and suffering Country, to its former happy condition of unity and peace.

In witness whereof, I have hereunto set my hand and caused the seal of the United States to be affixed.

Done at the City of Washington, this thirtieth day of March, in the year of our Lord one thousand eight hundred and sixty-three, and of the Independence of the United States the eighty seventh.

By the President: Abraham Lincoln

William H. Seward, Secretary of State.

It's been said that 'Confession is good for the soul,' because it leads to a recognition of wrongdoing, and a cleansing of the heart and conscience. Confession is also good for the National Collective Soul – for the same reasons. It results in re-orienting our moral compasses as individuals and nations.

GOD used the word 'measure' in terms of Israel's judgment in the past:

> "Behold, it is written before ME; 'I will not keep silence, but will repay – even repay into their bosom – **your iniquities and the iniquities of your fathers together**,' says THE LORD, who have burned incense on the mountains and blasphemed ME on the hills; Therefore **I will measure their former work into their bosom**." (ISAIAH 65:6,7 NKJV)

The moral State of Israel today is much like all nations: **CORRUPT**! Israelis suffer from addictions to drugs, alcohol, food, and pornography. Abortion is legal in Israel, but thankfully with more significant restrictions that in most Western nations. The

Divorce rate in Israel is on an upward trend in the last five years. But there is an ancient remedy given by GOD ALMIGHTY:

"If MY people who are called by MY NAME will humble themselves, and pray and seek MY FACE, and turn from their wicked ways; then I will hear from heaven, and **will forgive their sin and heal their land**." (II CHRONICLES 7:14 NKJV)

This 3rd vision given to Zechariah calls for the 'moral measurement' of Israel in the days leading up to Christ's return (ZECHARIAH 2:1,2,10), and finds them deserving of punishment by invading armies.

CHAPTER 13

ZECHARIAH'S 4TH & 5TH VISIONS: 2 WITNESSES

In a free society, discourse from every view-point is encouraged and practiced in schools, churches, the press, on the campaign trail, and in the halls of governance.

But in a tyrannical system of government like that of the coming 'Beast,' any opposing views and actions are systematically squashed!

Knowing this is the case, **GOD ALMIGHTY is going to make sure HIS VOICE is heard during the oppressive reign of this Despot**. That's why we read in the 11th chapter of the book of Revelation, that HE is going to raise up two men as HIS WITNESSES during the 42-month reign of 'the Beast':

"**And I** (THE LORD) **will give power to MY 2 Witnesses**, and they will prophesy 1260 days (parallel with the 42 month reign of 'the Beast' – Rev.13:5), clothed in sackcloth. These are the 2 Olive trees and the 2 lampstands (a clue to their identity) standing before THE GOD of THE EARTH. And if anyone wants to harm them, **fire proceeds from their mouth and devours their enemies**. And if anyone wants to harm them, he must be killed in this manner. **These have power to shut heaven, so that no rain falls in the days of their prophecy**; and they have powers over waters to turn them to blood, and to strike the earth with all plagues, as often as they desire. **When they finish their testimony, 'the Beast' that ascends out of the bottomless pit will make war against them, overcome them, and kill them.** And their dead bodies will lie in the street of the great city which spiritually is called 'Sodom' and 'Egypt,' where also our Lord (Jesus) was crucified (Jerusalem). **Then those from the peoples, tribes, tongues, and nations will see their dead bodies 3 ½ days, and not allow their dead bodies to be put into graves.** And those who dwell on the earth will rejoice over them, make merry, and send gifts to one another, because these 2 prophets tormented those who dwell on the earth. **Now after the 3 ½ days the breath of life from GOD entered them**, and they stood on their feet, and great fear fell on those who saw them. And they heard a loud voice from heaven saying to them, 'Come up here.' **And they ascended to heaven in a cloud, and their enemies saw them.**" (REVELATION 11:3-12 NKJV)

As Moses and Aaron worked miracles in the presence of Pharaoh of Egypt, these 2 Witnesses will have the power to control the weather and bring similar plagues upon 'the Beast' and his followers, confounding the 'learned' of the world who disparage religion and miracles as mere myth!

Witnessing involves a message, and even though we're not told any specifics of that message – it's safe to say that these two prophets will tell the world they're being misled by 'the Beast,' and that **the Bible is the only true source of revelation from the ONLY TRUE GOD!**

We're told by the Apostle Paul that there will be **a falling away** (from Christianity – II Thes.2:3) and that many Christians will be deceived by this blasphemous leader, '**because they did not receive the love of the truth**' (The Bible is truth John 17:17) - and will believe 'the lie' which may very well be that there is some other source of truth (the Quran).

THE IDENTITY OF THE 2 WITNESSES

Who will be the 2 Witnesses of GOD ALMIGHTY in the final days of this Age? It may shock you to hear that your Bible tells us precisely who these representatives of GOD will be – in fact, it gives us their names!

Take the time to read chapters 3 and 4 of the prophet Zechariah, where you'll find the 4th and 5th visions given to this Prophet. Then compare these two visions with the 11th chapter of the book of Revelation, verses 3-12, and you'll see that they are parallel chapters – both discussing the 2 Witnesses.

Remember that Revelation chapter 11 refers to the 2 Witnesses symbolically as the '**2 olive trees**' and the '**2 lampstands**' (Revelation 11:4). It also refers to them as '**standing before THE GOD of THE EARTH**' (11:4).

Only in one other place in your Bible do we find these same symbols together:

"Now the Angel who talked with me (Zechariah) came back and wakened me, as a man who is wakened out of his sleep. And he said to me, 'What do you see?' So I said, 'I am looking, and there is **a lampstand of solid gold with a bowl on top of it**, and on the stand 7 lamps with 7 pipes to the 7 lamps. 2

Olive trees are by it, one at the right of the bowl and the other at its left… And I further answered and said to him, '**What are these 2 Olive branches that drip into the receptacles of the 2 gold pipes from which the golden oil drains?**' … So he said, 'These are the 2 anointed ones, who stand beside THE LORD of THE WHOLE EARTH." (ZECHARIAH 4:1-3, 12,14 NKJV)

In both Revelation chapter 11 and Zechariah chapter 4, **these two servants of GOD 'stand before or beside THE LORD of THE EARTH' – and in both texts, they are symbolized by Olive trees or branches and lampstands or two pipes of a single lampstand** – meaning that the reader is supposed to equate the two individuals in both texts as the same servants.

The context of these symbols in chapters 3 and 4 of the book of Zechariah, is referring to historical individuals who shared the common task of guiding the rebuilding of Jerusalem and the Temple after Israel's return from captivity. **Joshua the High Priest** (whose name is synonymous with Jesus, meaning "YAH is Salvation') and **Zerubbabel** (whose name means: 'A stranger at Babylon, Dispersion of Confusion') were 2 of the leaders you read about in the books of Ezra and Nehemiah, which record the history of the 'post captivity' rebuilding and re-establishment of Judah as a nation.

ZECHARIAH'S 4TH VISION

The prophet Zechariah is given a 4th vision by GOD showing Joshua the High Priest standing before the Angel of THE LORD, his filthy clothes (symbolic of his sins 3:4) replaced with clean clothes, and the Angel giving him this message:

"If you will walk in MY ways, and if you will keep MY command, **then you shall also judge MY house**, and likewise have charge of MY courts; I will give you places to walk among those who stand here (GOD'S THRONE)." (ZECHARIAH 3:7 NKJV)

This is a vision of the future, for Joshua was already at the time of Zechariah's writing taking charge of the physical house of GOD and its courts (EZRA 3:2).

The Apostle Paul made clear that the Church is now the House or Temple of GOD (I Cor.3:16), and that '**the time has come for judgment to begin at the House of GOD**' (I PETER 4:17).

Zechariah seems to be saying that **Joshua, the High Priest** has a future commission involving a future **House of GOD** (The Church), and that if he is faithful in this new assignment, he will walk among the Angels he is standing with in the vision.

ZECHARIAH'S 5TH VISION

Zerubbabel, the Governor of the returning captives to rebuild Jerusalem and the Temple, is also mentioned within the context of **the Olive Trees and Lampstand pipes. Zechariah is given a 5th vision about these symbols**, prompting him to ask the Angel of THE LORD:

"… 'What are these my Lord?' Then the Angel who talked with me answered and said to me… 'This is the word of THE LORD to Zerubbabel: 'Not by (personal) might nor by (personal) power, but by MY SPIRIT,' says THE LORD of HOSTS. **Who are you**, **O great mountain? Before Zerubbabel you shall become a plain**! And he shall bring forth the capstone with shouts of 'Grace, grace to it!' The hands of Zerubbabel have laid the foundation of this temple; His hands shall also finish it.'" (ZECHARIAH 4:4-9)

Turning a mountain into a plain is a miracle of the tallest order. Yet we don't read anywhere in the books of Ezra and Nehemiah that Zerubbabel ever worked any miracles in his lifetime. But we just read that the 2 Witnesses, who are symbolized by the same olive trees and lampstands as Zerubbabel and Joshua - will work great miracles during the reign of 'the Beast!'

The prophet Haggai, who was also sent to prophesy and stir up those who went back to rebuild Jerusalem and the Temple, was told by GOD:

> "Speak to Zerubbabel, Governor of Judah, saying: '**I will shake heaven and earth**. I will overthrow the throne of kingdoms; **I will destroy the strength of the Gentile Kingdoms**; I will overthrow the chariots and those who ride in them; The horses and their riders shall come down, everyone by the sword of his brother. '**In that Day**,' says THE LORD of HOSTS, '**I will take you, Zerubbabel** MY servant, the son of Shealtiel,' says THE LORD, **and will make you like a signet ring**; for I have chosen you,' says THE LORD of HOSTS.'" (HAGGAI 2:21-23 NKJV)

Remember it's the **Gentile Kingdoms** that tread the Holy City (Jerusalem) underfoot for 42 months (REVELATION 11:2) – the same reign as 'the Beast.'

And immediately after the 2 Witnesses ascend to heaven, after being dead for 3 ½ days, there's a **great earthquake** (Rev.11:13) as described by the Prophet Haggai.

The giving of the 'signet ring' is an excellent act of empower-ment, as in the case of Pharaoh giving his to Joseph (GEN.41:42), and the King of Persia giving his to Mordecai (ESTHER 8:2).

The fact that Haggai is told that Zerubbabel will be made like **the signet ring** of GOD ALMIGHTY 'in that Day' – indicates that HE is going to raise up Zerubbabel from the grave to be one of the two witnesses along with Joshua, the former High Priest! These 2 men will not only witness against 'the Beast' and his followers, they will judge and help prepare the House of GOD (the Church), to become the Bride of Jesus Christ (REV.19:7)!

CHRISTIANITY is currently a Religion divided into thousands of opposing views. But ALMIGHTY GOD will use the 2 Witnesses to unite Christians of all denominations so that we finally ful-fill the Apostle Paul's command to 'All speak the same thing!' (I Corinthians 1:10)

And the Muslim world, led by the Beast and False Prophet (Revelation 19:20), will be forced to listen to an alternative mes-sage from THE ONLY TRUE GOD THE FATHER (John 17:3), given through HIS 2 Witnesses, Joshua and Zerubbabel!

CHAPTER 14

THE 6TH VISION 'THE FLYING SCROLL'

The 5th chapter of the book of Revelation and the 5th chapter of the book of Zechariah are 'parallel chapters' in that they both begin with a vision of a Scroll:

> "And I (John) saw in the right hand of HIM who sat on the throne – **a scroll written inside and on the back**, sealed with 7 seals. Then I saw a strong angel proclaiming with a loud voice, 'Who is worthy to open the scroll and to loose its seals?' (REV.5:1,2)

> "Then I turned and raised my eyes, and saw there **a flying scroll**. And he (the Angel of the Lord) said to me, 'What do you see?' So I answered, 'I see a flying scroll. Its length is 20 cubits and its width 10 cubits.' Then he said to me, 'This is **the curse** that goes out over the face of the whole earth: '**Every thief shall be expelled**,' according to this side of the scroll; and '**Every perjurer shall be expelled**.' according to the other side of it. 'I will send out the curse,' says THE LORD of HOSTS; it shall enter the house of the thief and the house of the one who swears

falsely by MY NAME. **It shall remain in the midst of his house and consume it, with its timber and stones.**" (ZECHARIAH 5:1-4 NKJV)

This is Zechariah's 6th Vision. Notice that the visions given to both John and Zechariah involve a scroll written on both sides, unlike any other scrolls mentioned in your Bible. This is meant to show the reader that they are one and the same scroll - being seen by two Prophets of two different Eras. A few details are different in the two visions, in that Zechariah sees the scroll flying through the air, while John comments that the scroll is sealed with 7 Seals.

As you can see, this scroll unleashes a curse upon **thieves and perjurers**, which results in the cursed being purged, killed by a plague that even takes over their houses!

This 'curse' may be generated when the 4th of the '7 Seals' upon the Scroll is opened. The Apostle John sees someone riding on a pale horse whose name is 'Death.' This is most likely representative of pestilence that puts people who contract it into an early grave (Gk. Hades Rev.6:8).

The' curse' that accompanies the flying scroll that Zechariah sees in his vision - must also be pestilence – because it enters into the house of the one cursed - infecting the very stone and timber of the dwelling place!

Only one other place in Scripture do we find mention of something entering 'timber and stones' of people's houses – and it's the disease of leprosy, also known as Hansen's Disease:

"Now if the plague comes back and breaks out in the house, after he has taken away the stones, after he has scraped the house, and after it is plastered, then the priest shall come and look; and if indeed the plague has spread in the house, **it is an active leprosy in the house**. It is unclean. And **he shall break down the house**, **its stones**, **its timber**, and all the plaster of the house, and he shall carry them outside the city to an unclean place." (LEVITICUS 14:43-45 NKJV)

This is scary stuff – far more deadly than COVID-19 or the Spanish Flu, and far more devastating in that it infects the whole house, making it uninhabitable!

This text also describes what this contagion looks like when it is infused within building materials:

"And he (the priest) shall examine the plague (leprosy); and indeed if the plague is on the walls of the house with **ingrained streaks**, **greenish or reddish**, **which appear to be deep in the wall**, then the priest shall go out of the house, and shut up the house 7 days. And the priest shall come again on the 7th day and look; and indeed if the plague has spread on the walls of the house, then the priest shall command that they take away the stones in which is the plague, and they shall cast them into an unclean place outside the city. And he shall cause the house to be scraped inside, all around, and the dust that they scrape off they shall pour out in an unclean place outside the city. Then they shall take other stones and put them in the place of those stones, and he shall take other mortar and plaster the house." (LEVITICUS 14:37-42 NKJV)

What a terrible curse this is! Those who got it were quarantined outside the camp, sometimes for the rest of their lives! And like a mold that permeates sheetrock in modern-day houses – it must be removed to make the house habitable once again.

Don't think of leprosy as some ancient plague of the past that has been eradicated from the earth. In a span of a little over 100 years, some 8500 leprous men, women, and children were forced into isolation on the Hawaiian island of Molokai, in the late 1800s, from 1850 to 1969.

Leprosy affects the nervous system, resulting in numbness in the hands and feet. It manifests itself in discolored patches of skin, loss of eyebrows and eyelashes, lumps on the face and earlobes, and ulcers on the soles of feet.

Will GOD ALMIGHTY bring the plague of leprosy upon Human Beings when the 4th seal of the double-sided flying scroll is opened, and the Horseman called 'Death' rides forth upon the earth?

It appears so – since the Scroll's curse enters timber and stones of the cursed's home, something only 'leprosy' is described in your Bible as spreading in this manner!

THE TARGET OF THIS CURSE

The Prophet Zechariah is told that **this curse** (of leprosy) **goes out over the face of the whole earth resulting in the purging of thieves and perjurers** from the ranks of the living.

Theft comes in many forms: Most of Humanity has stolen GOD'S SOVEREIGNTY away from HIM in taking the right to de-cide for themselves what's right and wrong; People who use GOD'S NAME in cursing, steal the reverence due HIM; Those who ignore HIS command to cease work in order to gather and worship HIM, steal this DIVINE APPOINTMENT away from their CREATOR; Children can steal the reverence and honor their parents are due; someone can steal the life of another person, and all that love him or her; someone who commits adultery, is stealing the mate of someone else; someone who bears false witness, is stealing the honor and integrity of another person; and coveting someone else's property, is spiritual theft. In short, theft is involved in breaking all of the 10 commandments, becoming a kind of summary word for what GOD wants us to avoid in our relationships with HIM and our fellow man.

Perjury is theft in the Courtroom. If someone lies 'under oath,' he or she has violated not only the 9th commandment against bearing false witness – but also the 3rd commandment in placing their hand on a Bible and swearing to tell the truth, '**so help me GOD!**' A perjurer has also violated the 8th commandment, having stolen truth and justice in a court proceeding!

The underlying principle behind the 10 COMMANDMENTS is REVERENCE for GOD and one's neighbor. The thief and perjurer are filled with IRREVERENCE – and their CREATOR is going to exact HIS VENGEANCE upon them through the Flying Scroll curse of leprosy!

AN ADJOINING TEXT

There is a text in your Bible that illustrates the breaking of both the 3rd and 8th commandments simultaneously:

"Therefore behold, I am against the Prophets,' says THE LORD, **who steal MY words everyone from his neighbor**. Behold, I am against the Prophets, says THE LORD, **who use their tongues**

and say, 'HE says.' Behold, I am against **those who prophesy false dreams,'** says THE LORD, 'and tell them, **and cause MY people to err by their lies** and by their recklessness. Yet I did not send them or command them; therefore they shall not profit this people at all,' says THE LORD… for you have perverted the words of THE LIVING GOD, THE LORD of HOSTS, our GOD." (JEREMIAH 23:30-32 NKJV)

A Human Being can perjure him or herself (render oneself guilty of swearing falsely in GOD'S NAME), by saying, 'The Lord told me…' when THE LORD has not spoken to them at all! Then others steal their words and pass them on as if THE LORD has spoken – when HE hasn't!

The '**Flying Scroll Curse**' of leprosy will come upon those **who steal words** from their fellow man (who claim to speak for GOD) **swearing falsely** that these words are from THE LORD!

I cringe when I hear people say that 'THE LORD told me this or that,' and then others pass it on as GOSPEL. Where is the wisdom and humility in that?

There are people all over the internet claiming that GOD ALMIGHTY has spoken to them, when HE hasn't, and have thousands of followers who happily spread their lies. These people are thieves in that they steal words from one another, swearing falsely that their shared message is from GOD HIMSELF!

People who tell others that GOD has told them something (when HE hasn't) are misappropriating GOD'S SOVEREIGNTY! Shouldn't we instead just stick with the WRITTEN word of GOD, when we want to share GOD'S word?

Don't bring the 'Flying Scroll Curse' upon yourself or your household! Rather do as James, the brother of Jesus was inspired to write:

"For what is your life? It is even a vapor that appears for a little time and then vanishes away. **Instead you ought to say**, '**If THE LORD WILLS**, **we shall live and do this or that**.' But now you boast in your arrogance. All such boasting is evil. Therefore, to him who knows to do good and does not do it, to him it is SIN." (JAMES 4:14-17 NKJV)

"See then that you walk circumspectly, not as fools but as wise…" (EPHESIANS 5:15 NKJV)

Good advice from the brother of Jesus (James), and the Apostle Paul. May we all heed it!

CHAPTER 15
THE 8TH VISION: 'THE 4 HORSEMEN'

The masses of Humanity love a good treasure hunt, and avidly drive to the local theatre to watch Indiana Jones decipher signs and symbols in his journey to unearth another ancient artifact! Millions of Newspaper readers also bend their brains every day in figuring out crossword puzzles.

GOD THE FATHER says:

"..If you receive MY words, and treasure MY commands within you, so that you incline your ear to wisdom, and apply your heart to understanding; Yes if you cry out for discernment, and lift up your voice for understanding, if you seek her as silver, and search for her as for hidden treasures; **then you will understand the fear of THE LORD, and find the knowledge of GOD**." (PROVERBS 2:1-5 NKJV)

One of the reasons so few Christians understand their Bibles is that they don't search it and study it with the same passion they would if they were on a treasure hunt, or with the same focus they give to solving word-puzzles, or with the same enthusiasm that moves them into a theatre to watch an archaeologist search for relics of the past!

When it comes to understanding Scripture, GOD ALMIGHTY purposely made it challenging, probably to see who would make it a priority, and who really longed for understanding. But also that we might cry out to HIM for illumination, and see that 'understanding' is not a solo process.

No book of the Bible has more signs, symbols, and puzzling characters, than the book of Revelation. And among its most enigmatic figures are the '**4 Horsemen of the Apocalypse**':

"Now I (John) saw when the Lamb (Jesus) opened one of the (7) Seals; and I heard one of the 4 living creatures saying with a voice like thunder, 'Come and see.' And I looked, and behold, **a white horse**. He who sat on it had a bow; and a crown was given to him, and he went out conquering and to conquer. When He opened the 2nd Seal, I heard the 2nd living creature saying, 'Come and see.' **Another horse, fiery red**, went out. And it was granted to the one who sat on it to take peace from the earth, and that people should kill one another; and there was given to him a great sword. When He opened the 3rd Seal, I heard the 3rd living creature say, 'Come and see.' So I looked, and behold, **a black horse**, and he who sat on it had a pair of scales in his hand. And I heard a voice in the midst of the 4 living creatures saying, 'A quart of wheat for a denarius, and 3 quarts of barley for a denarius; and do not harm the oil and the wine.' When He opened the 4th Seal, I heard the voice of the 4th living creature saying, 'Come and See.' So I looked, and behold, **a pale** (Gk. 'Khloros' - **green**) **horse**, and the name of him who sat on it was 'Death,' and hades followed with him. **And power was given to them over a ¼ of the earth, to kill with sword, with hunger, with death, and by the beasts of the earth**." (REVELATION 6:1-8 NKJV)

Everywhere else in Scripture, we find 'horsemen,' the text is very clearly speaking of the cavalry of national armies! (EXODUS 14:9; I KINGS 4:26)

The White and Red Horsemen ride to **conquer** and **take peace from the earth** – thus, they represent armies of nations. The only question is, what nations? Is there something about these Horsemen that points us to specific nations that are war-like in the 'Latter Days'?

The Black Horseman pictures scarcity and famine that leads to inflation on food – a common result of war.

The 4th Horse is described as 'Pale,' by most translators, probably because no one has ever seen a 'Green' horse. But the Greek word 'Khloros' is translated 'green grass' in Rev.8:7, and is the root word from which we get the English word, 'Chlorophyll' – the greening agent found in leaves and plants. The Horseman that rides the 'green horse,' is called 'Death,' and probably represents pestilence, also a common side effect of war.

THE SIGNIFICANCE OF THE 4 COLOR HORSEMEN

Lead Horsemen carry the flag symbolizing their nation or kingdom into battle. Those flags have colors and symbols on them that distinguish one people from another.

If you google the maps of the world, you'll find that **the 'national flags' that have the 4 colors of the 4 Horsemen today** (white, red, black, green) – **are Muslim Nations**! The one exception, is the flag of Kenya, a pre-dominantly Christian nation, which also has these 4 colors. However, the last two decades have seen a concerted effort by the Islamic population (11%) there, to assert themselves into the nation's social and political decision making processes. **Early on in 2020**, the Muslim terrorist group, Al-Shabaab, carried out five attacks in Kenya, including a Kenyan military base. It's very possible, with the way things are trending, that by the time the '4 Horseman' ride - Kenya will also be a Muslim nation!

In 1917 the British aided the Arabs in a revolt against the Ottoman Empire. The Arab Liberation Flag consisted of the 4 Colors of the 4 Horsemen, representing 4 different dynasties of Islamic History: White = The Umayyad Dynasty; Red = The Hashemite Dynasty; Black = The Abbasid Dynasty; and Green = The Fatimid Dynasty – and are also referred to as 'Pan Arab Colors.'

Nations with these 4 colors in their flags today include Afghanistan, Iraq, Jordan, Kuwait, Libya, Palestine, Sudan, Syria, and the United Arab Emirates – all Muslim majority nations to-day! Every other Muslim Nation in the Middle East has one or more of these colors in their national flags.

PARALLEL COLORED HORSES – ZECHARIAH'S 8TH VISION

People familiar with the 4 Horsemen, which make up the first 4 Seals that Christ Himself opens, may not be aware of a parallel chapter in their Bibles, which also describes horses of the same colors. The prophet Zechariah was given the following vision by GOD THE FATHER:

"Then I turned, and lifted up mine eyes, and looked, and behold, there came 4 chariots out from between 2 mountains, and the mountains were mountains of brass. **In the 1st chariot were red horses**; and **in the 2nd chariot black horses**; And **in the 3rd chariotwhite horses**; and in the **4th chariot grisled and bay** (Heb. 'Amots' of a **strong color**) **horses**. Then I answered and said unto the Angel that talked with me, 'What are these my sovereign?' And the Angel answered and said unto me, '**These are the 4 spirits of the heavens**, which go forth from standing before THE SOVEREIGN of ALL THE EARTH. The black horses which are therein go forth into the North country, and the white go forth after them; and the grisled go forth toward the South country. And the bay went forth, and sought to go that they might walk to and fro through the earth: and he said, 'Get you hence, walk to and fro through the earth' So they walked to and fro through the earth. Then cried he (the Angel) upon me, 'Behold, these that go toward the North country have quieted my spirit in the North country.'" (ZECHARIAH 6:1-8 KJV)

This is the 8th and final vision given to Zechariah. It is similar to the 1st in that it involves horses, and that it culminates in a quieting of the Angel's spirit in the North (Home to Gog and the King of the North).

The eerie similarity of the colors of the horses pulling these chariots, with the 4 Horsemen of John's vision (Rev.6), is meant to purposefully lead the reader to connect them in some way. Both texts describe white, red, and black horses. The 4th Horseman of Revelation six is green (a strong color used in traffic lights). The

4th set of horses leading the chariots of Zechariah's vision are described as 'grisled' (a grayish tone) and 'bay' (of a strong color). That strong color could be 'green' just like the 4th horseman.

The difference between the two texts is that the 4 Horsemen ride during the Great Tribulation, with war, famine, and pestilence accompanying them - while the 4 chariots ride after the Battle of Armageddon, in a kind of reconnaissance mission that reports back of tranquility in the region of the North – where the 'King of the North' has been vanquished in the Battle of Armageddon. This is the 2nd Rest we talked about in chapter 5 of this book, about the 'COVID-19 EFFECT.'

THE OVERLOOKED 5TH COLOR

There's a 5th color mentioned in Zechariah's vision that has been mostly overlooked by prophetic pundits:

> "Then I turned and raised my eyes and looked, and behold, 4 chariots were coming from between 2 mountains, and the mountains were mountains of **bronze**. (ZECHARIAH 6:1)

As mentioned previously, mountains are symbolic of kingdoms in several Biblical texts. And there's only one kingdom anywhere in your Bible that is associated with the color bronze:

> "But after you (King Nebuchadnezzar) shall arise another kingdom inferior to yours; then another, **a third kingdom of bronze**, which shall rule over all the earth." (DANIEL 2:39)

King Nebuchadnezzar dreamed of a great image with a head of gold, its chest and arms of silver, its belly, and thighs of bronze, its legs of iron, its feet partly of iron and partly of clay.

Daniel, the prophet, interprets the dream, showing the King that the image represents 4 great kingdoms, the first 3 in succession, the 4th somewhere down the line of history. We know from history that Nebuchadnezzar's Babylonian empire was followed by the Medo-Persian Empire, which was followed by Alexander the Great's Greek Empire.

So **the Greek Empire** was this 3rd '**kingdom of bronze**.' And we know that after Alexander's death, his kingdom was divided among his 4 Generals, which became 4 separate mountains or kingdoms. Zechariah is told in this 8th vision that the 4 colored chariots were coming from between 2 mountains of bronze (or 2 of these 4 divisions of Alexander's empire). The direction that the chariots ride are north and south (Zechariah 6:6), pointing to the King of the North and the King of the South.

ALMIGHTY GOD, the ONE WHO **FORETOLD** all these things, sends out chariots led by horses of the same color as **the 4 Horsemen of the Apocalypse**, to let us know that the nations represented by the colors of those horses (Arab nations of the Middle East, **ride with the bronze mountains** representing the 'King of the North' and the 'King of the South'!

HE also wants us to take comfort in the fact that although the 4 Horsemen wreak havoc on the world – their ride will be short-lived – followed by the ride of the 4 chariots of the same colors (steered by Angels), who report that the earth is once more resting quietly after the Beast's armies are destroyed at the Battle of Armageddon!

CHAPTER 16
NATIONAL FAMILY FEUDS

Most Americans have heard of the famous feud between the 'Hatfields and McCoys' – 2 families that lived in the West Virginia – Kentucky area, during and after the Civil War in this country. The feud is so famous that it's invoked in reference to any kind of turbulent conflagration between two opposing parties.

Asa McCoy fought for the Union Army and was murdered by a group of Confederate men while returning home from the war. Anse Hatfield was suspected to be among the murderers but was cleared when it was confirmed that he'd been homesick. Over time, it began to be believed that Anse's uncle was the real killer.

A second event that stirred up strife between the two families was over the ownership of a certain hog, which both families claimed ownership of.

And in the spirit of 'all's fair in love and war,' the feud escalated when Roseanna McCoy entered into a relationship with Anse Hatfield's son.

The feud claimed more than a dozen lives of the two families, and resulted in trials that lasted two decades.

A world-impacting 'Family Feud'

As bad as all these sound, it doesn't come close to the greatest family feud in Human History, which has lasted not just decades, nor centuries, but for millennia!

The feud which developed between the sons of Abraham: Isaac and Ishmael, and his grandsons: Jacob (Israel) and Esau, grew into National quarrels that still thrive today!

Most are aware that Israel was made up of 12 tribes that became a union of states in ancient Israel. But most are not aware of the 12 tribes of Ishmael:

"These were the sons of Ishmael, and these are the names of **the 12 tribal rulers according to their settlements and camps**... His descendants settled in the area from Havilah to Shur (Arabian Peninsula), near the eastern border of Egypt, as you go toward Ashur (Northern Iraq). **They lived in hostility toward all the tribes related to them**. (GENESIS 25:16 NIV)

"**He** (Ish'mael) **shall be a wild man**; His hand shall be against every man, and every man's hand against him." (GENESIS 16:12 NKJV)

This prophetic feud among the ancestors of Ishmael has played out through centuries of conflict in all generations. There is an old Arab Bedouin saying: '**I against my brothers. I and my brothers against my cousins. I and my brothers and my cousins against the world**."

It's that last phrase in the saying that is invoked against common enemies - like Israel.

Political Analyst, K.T. McFarland, conveyed her understanding of this feuding family grown large when she wrote about the United States war in Iraq:

"After one of the longest lasting wars in American History we have little to show for the thousands of American deaths; Tens of thousands of American casualties and trillions in spent American treasure. Why? Because we failed to realize one essential truth of the Middle East – that the nations in that part of the world just aren't like us.

We in the West think of peace as Society's default position. War is a temporary state of affairs that happens when peace fails. For us, war is something that has a beginning, middle, and an end. When it is over, win or lose, the warring factions lay down their arms, and resume their normal lives.

In the modern Middle East, **war and peace are seen through a different lens**. **War is the default position**, **the normal state of affairs**. Peace is what happens between wars; it is the temporary pause where defeated factions fade into the woodwork to lie low, regroup, and plan their next assault." (The Sad Truth about America and Iraq, K.T. Mcfarland, Fox News January 6th, 2014)

Even a Super-Power Nation like the United States can't force PEACE upon peoples with a centuries-old paradigm of WAR and CONFLICT as THE NORM. Unfortunately, we've had to find this out through the painful experience of trying to arbitrate between warring factions of people who share the same religion, and in great measure, the same DNA family lines!

This centuries-old Arab Tribal infighting pales into insignificance the decades long quarrel between the Hatfields and McCoys.

FEUDING COUSINS

Simultaneous with this Intra-Family Feud of the Arabs – has been the sibling wars between Israel and his step-brother Ishmael's descendants, among them 'Palestinians.'

Added to it is the conflict between Isaac's two sons, Jacob (whose name was changed to Israel), and Esau, his twin brother, who struggled with one another in the womb! (GEN.25:22)

When their mother Rebekah experienced this struggle, she went to inquire of THE LORD about it, and HE said:

"**2 nations are in your womb**, 2 peoples shall be separated from your body; One people shall be stronger than the other, **and the older shall serve the younger**." (GEN.25:23 NKJV)

Most Christians know the infamous story of the younger son Jacob bribing his older brother Esau for his birthright, with a bowl of lentils, after Esau had come back from a hunt, famished in hunger.

And most Christians know how Jacob's mom Rachel schemed to formally take Esau's birthright blessing from him, by disguising Jacob as Esau in the presence of her nearly blind husband, Isaac.

The animosity that developed between the brothers over these incidents became an on-going rift between their descendants, right up to the present day.

To make things worse, Esau married into his uncle Ishmael's family line (GENESIS 28:9), and the envy and anger against Israel and his descendants multiplied exponentially!

Ancient Animosity

The ancient hatred toward Israel, by her step-brother and cousins, which now flows from millions of descendants - **is condemned by GOD ALMIGHTY throughout the Scripture**:

"**So Esau hated Jacob** because of the blessing with which his father blessed him, and Esau said in his heart, 'The days of morning for my father are at hand; then **I will kill my brother Jacob**." (GENESIS 27:41 NKJV)

"…Our sister (Rebekah, may you become the mother of thousands of ten thousands; and may your descendants (Israelites) possess the gates **of those who hate them**." (GENESIS 24:60 NKJV)

"O GOD, **the nations have come into your inheritance**, YOUR holy temple they have defiled; they have laid Jerusalem in heaps. The dead bodies of YOUR servants they have given as food for the birds of heavens, the flesh of your saints to the beasts of the earth. Their blood they have shed like water all around Jerusalem, and there was no one to bury them. **We have become a reproach to our neighbors**, a scorn and derision to those who are around us** (Arabs, children of Lot, Esau)." (PSALM 79:1-4 NKJV)

"On the day that **the enemies of the Jews** (Persians) had hoped to overpower them, the opposite occurred, in that the Jews themselves overpowered **those who hated them**." (ESTHER 9:1 NKJV)

"Thus says THE LORD GOD: '**Because the Philistines dealt vengefully** and took vengeance with a spiteful heart, **to destroy because of the old hatred**,' therefore thus says THE LORD GOD: '**I will stretch out MY HAND against the Philistines**, and I will cut off the Cherethites and destroy the remnant of the seacoast (Modern Day Gaza)." (EZEKIEL 25:15,16 NKJV)

"Thus says THE LORD GOD: 'Behold O Mount Seir (habitation of **Esau's progeny**) I am against you; I will stretch out MY HAND against you, and make you desolate… **because you have had an ancient hatred, and have shed the blood of the children of Israel**…" (EZEKIEL 35:3,5)

"For 3 transgressions of Edom (**Esau**), and for 4, I will not turn away its punishment, **because he pursued his brother** (Jacob – Israel) **with the sword**, and cast off all pity; **His anger tore perpetually, and he kept his wrath forever**." (AMOS 1:11 NKJV)

This hatred of the Jews is not some ancient venom that has dried up in the wind. It continues to manifest itself in taunting existential threats against the State of Israel today:

"Anybody who recognizes Israel will burn in the fire of the Islamic nation's (Iran's) fury, any who recognizes the Zionist regime means he is acknowledging the surrender and defeat of the Islamic World… As the Imam (Ayatollah Ruhollah Khomeini) said, 'Israel must be wiped off the map.'" (Mahmoud Ahmadinejab, President of Iran, 2005-2017 at a Conference titled: 'The World Without Zionism')

"I am not talking about regular body parts. I tell the Israelis, we have the heads of your soldiers, we have hands, we have legs." (Hezbollah's leader: Sheik Hassan Nasrallah after 2006 war against Israel)

"Israel's allies cannot insure the survival of the Zionist Regime, and the strategic depth of Palestinian resistance will defeat Israel." (Mohammad Bagheri, Iranian Military leader, on Iran's Quds - Jerusalem in the hands of Muslims – Day, 2020)

"In June, Syrian boxer Ala Ghasoun refused to participate in a (2016) Olympic qualifying match against an Israeli, saying that to do so 'would mean that I, as an athlete, and Syria, as a State, recognize the State of Israel. I quit the competition because my rival was Israeli, and I cannot shake his hand or compete against him while he represents a Zionist regime, that kills the Syrian people,' Mr. Ghasoun said in Arab media, according to Jerusalem's i24 News." (The Washington Times, Valerie Richardson August 10th, 2016)

Every murder of an individual, and every attempt at Genocide against a people, has a motive. The motive here is clear – an 'Ancient Hatred' of Israeli's - that gets passed on from generation to generation in the Arab world!

And how is this hatred passed on? One way is through the UNRWA (United Nations Relief and Works Agency), which in 2013 sponsored a Palestinian children's program called 'Camp Jihad.' Video from this camp obtained by a news agency called 'The Times' of Israel, shows that these children are being taught that "Jews are the wolf," and that one day Palestinians will conquer Israeli cities by force:

"I will defeat the Jews, they are a gang of infidels and Christians. They don't like Allah and do not worship Allah. And they hate us." (a camper named Tayma told the video crew making the documentary)

Another method of indoctrinating kids to hate Jews in Muslim nations is through their schools:

"According to a (U.S.) State Department funded-study, assorted religious schools have adopted Saudi State Textbooks in a variety of countries around the world. These texts were even adopted at one point in territory controlled by ISIS... Despite claims of comprehensive reform in this area, we found that the kingdom's 2018-2019 curriculum still encouraged hatred or violence against Jews, Christians, Shi'ite Muslims, women, gay men, and anybody who converts away from Islam. All were subjected to some degrading or dehumanizing characterizations and described as targets for violence." (Forward Magazine, David Andrew Weinberg, November 4, 2019)

According to your Bible – **Israel is the 'Apple of GOD'S EYE.'** (DEUTERONOMY 32:10) (ZECHARIAH 2:8). Those who bless it are blessed, and those who curse it are cursed! (GENESIS 12:3) (NUMBERS 24:9).

GOD is going to take HIS PROTECTION away from Israel in the days ahead (ISAIAH 22:8), because they have copied the sins of the nations of this world, instead of learning from their forefathers' mistakes, and walking by the word of GOD given through them.

But woe to those nations who rejoice in Her demise, who pummel and plunder Her in the name of a foreign god! (OBADIAH 11-16)

CHAPTER 17
'THE WATCHMAN'

The Prophet Ezekiel was given VISIONS of what would happen to the House of Israel (The 10 Northern Tribes which separated from the House of Judah – I KINGS 12:30,31), which had been taken captive by the Assyrian king Shalmaneser V in 721 BCE – about a century before Ezekiel was born:

> "So THE SPIRIT lifted me up and took me away… Then I came to the captives at Tel Abib (Northern Syrian today), who dwelt by the river Chebar; and I (Ezekiel) sat where they sat, and remained there astonished among them 7 days. Now it came to pass at the end of 7 days that the word of THE LORD came to me, saying, 'Son of man, I have made you **a watchman** for the House of Israel; therefore hear a word from MY MOUTH, and give them warning from ME: When I say to the wicked, 'You shall surely die,' and you give him no warning, nor speak to warn the wicked from his wicked way, to save his life, that same wicked man shall die in his iniquity; **but his blood I will require at your hand. Yet if you warn the wicked**, and he does not turn from his wickedness, nor from his wicked way, he shall die in his iniquity; but **you have delivered your soul**." (EZEKIEL 3:14-19 NKJV)

Ezekiel was given the commission of a watchman! And he received a message from GOD that he was to pass onto the House of Israel, about the length of their captivity:

"Lie also on your left side, and lay the iniquity of the '**House of Israel**' upon it… For I have laid on you **the years of their iniquity, according to the number of days, 390 days**; so you shall bear the iniquity of the 'House of Israel.' (EZEKIEL 4:4,5 NKJV)

The 'House of Israel,' as mentioned, was taken captive by King Shalmaneser V in 721 BCE. 390 years later, Alexander the Great defeated the Medes & Persians, enabling the descendants of these lost 10 Tribes to leave their captivity and migrate north into Europe. Ezekiel's symbolic act of lying 390 days on his left side translated into exactly 390 years punishment for Israel – something only GOD could have brought about!

Jesus said to His disciples:

"**Watch therefore**, and pray always that you may be counted worthy to escape all these things (prophecies: some of which are shared in this book), that will come to pass, and to stand before the Son of Man." (LUKE 21:36 NKJV)

Jesus gave His followers the commission of a 'Watchman!' Christians need to keep a watchful eye on world events and how they relate to prophesy – so they can warn people of what is prophesied to come. If Christians fail to warn others, then the blood of their family, friends, and neighbors will be on their heads in GOD'S SIGHT – because Jesus commanded His followers to WATCH, and the Apostle Paul admonished us to WARN (Col.1:28)!

Ezekiel was told by THE LORD to instruct the people of Israel to place **Watchmen** on the City walls to warn the people of impending danger:

"…Son of man, speak to the children of your people, and say to them: 'When I bring the sword upon a land, and the people of the land take a man from their territory and make him their **watchman, when he sees the sword** (armies) **coming upon the land, if he blows the trumpet and warns the people, then whoever hears the sound of the trumpet and does not take warning,** if the sword comes and takes him away, **his blood shall be on his own head**. He heard the sound of the trumpet, but did not take warning; his blood shall be upon himself. **But he who takes warning will save his life**." (EZEKIEL 33:1-5 NKJV)

A SWORD symbolizes WARFARE in your Bible, and the TRUMPET was like a modern-day SIREN that goes off at noon in Small Town America – a sort of trial run to have a means of warning people when a Tornado or anything else threatened the town.

So on the parapet of a walled city like Jerusalem – they would post a WATCHMAN who was furnished with a TRUMPET – and if he could see a plume of dust off in the distance – his job was to blow the TRUMPET and WARN the people of an invading army coming towards the city!

If you look in the book of NUMBERS chapter 10 – **the Nation of Israel moved, or camped** and **pitched their tents according to specific TRUMPET CALLS**. They also used TRUMPETS to call an Assembly of the people or their leaders… **but there was one blast of the TRUMPET that stood out from all the others – they all knew what an ALARM sounded like** – those people of that day knew what it meant when a TRUMPET ALARM was blown. That rapid and shrill sound of the TRUMPET struck TERROR into the hearts of all those who heard it because they knew that it meant their city was about to be attacked!

Ezekiel said that when the Watchman blows the trumpet, and people ignore the warning - then it becomes his' or hers' responsibility to respond. They heard the Trumpet, they've been warned, – but some did nothing about it. They stayed right there, they didn't seek shelter, and like those who ignored Noah's warning, but took no action, they and their loved ones perished – when they could have lived, if they had repented and acknowledged the warning message! But sometimes you literally can't drag people away from impending danger! Remember that Angels had to drag Lot and his family out of Sodom to save their lives!

In the pages of this book, you've heard many warning messages from the Bible, about impending doom prophesied to come upon the world that JESUS called THE GREAT TRIBULATION. You've seen the prophecy given to the Prophet Zechariah describing **the COVID-19 EFFECT – the whole earth resting quietly**. You've seen that this is just the calm before the storm of events that will plunge this world into chaos and confusion.

Will you take action? Will you repent of your sins? Will you acknowledge that this warning message is from THE LORD HIMSELF – and save yourself and your family?

If not – THE LORD says that your blood, and the blood of your family - is on your own head!